The Battle of Massard Prairie

The 1864 Confederate Attacks on Fort Smith, Arkansas

by Dale Cox

Edited by William Cox

2008

ISBN: 978-0-6152-1590-7

A Yuchi Heritage Publication

William Cox, Publisher
4514 Oak Grove Road
Bascom, Florida 32423

Visit the author online at:

www.exploresouthernhistory.com

"Then the land had rest from war."

For Rebecca...

This book is respectfully dedicated to the people of Fort Smith, Arkansas. Thank you for receiving me with courtesy, hospitality and friendship.

Contents

Maps

Introduction

On July 27, 1864, Union and Confederate forces clashed on a broad prairie just outside the frontier city of Fort Smith, Arkansas. In the words of one eyewitness, it was "a right gallant little affair."

Although small in size, there is much about the Battle of Massard Prairie that recommends it for detailed study. The attack by Gano's Confederate cavalry was one of the last successful large mounted charges in American history and a brilliant example of the Napoleonic *beau sabre* ideal that had captivated military minds for much of the 19th century. Sweeping cavalry charges were dying by the time of the fight at Massard Prairie, driven bloodily into the past by advances in weaponry and tactics

In their attack on the 6th Kansas Cavalry, nearly 1,000 white and Native American Confederate horsemen swept across miles of open prairie and nearly annihilated a well-armed and seasoned Union force. The great mounted charge took place at a time when most cavalry fighting was done on foot, horses simply being used as transportation to get from one place to another. The open field fight at Massard Prairie, however, was one of the most complete Confederate victories of the war west of the Mississippi.

The battle was also unique because it was a highly effective action carried out by white and Native American soldiers fighting side by side. In addition, in resulted in one of the few documented cases of Union soldiers scalping Confederate dead after a battle.

The city of Fort Smith has grown dramatically over the last 143 years and Massard Prarie today retains little of its 1864 appearance. Commercial, residential and industrial development covers much of the battlefield, with the exception of a core parcel now preserved as the Massard Prairie Battlefield Park. From surrounding ridges, however, it is possible to look out over what once was a vast prairie and imagine it as it must have appeared to the soldiers of 1864.

On the pages that follow, I have attempted to reconstruct the Battle of Massard Prairie and related events as well as can be done considering the limited number of eyewitness accounts that survive. Some of the information is contradictory and it is possible for reasonable people to reach different conclusions from the same documentation. This narrative provides my interpretation of what happened at Massard Prairie on July 27, 1864, based on the available accounts and time spent exploring the ground itself.

This narrative is not intended to be the "final word" on the engagement, but rather a "first word" that hopefully will lead to additional research and future publications by other writers. I hope that future researchers can take the facts presented here and expand them to provide an even better understanding of the battle and subsequent Confederate attack on Fort Smith.

I also hope that this volume will inspire greater interest in the battlefield and its related sites among the public at large. The city of Fort Smith, concerned citizens and interested business leaders combined to preserve a key portion of the site where the battle was fought. With further development, Massard Prairie Battlefield Park could become a significant part of Fort Smith's developing heritage tourism industry.

My sincere gratitude is extended to everyone who assisted in the research and writing phases of this project. My special thanks are due to my son William. He has taken interest in the publication of my manuscripts and his assistance, time and efforts made this book possible.

A number of others assisted greatly in the completion of this publication. Randal Gilbert provided the photographs of Camp Ford that appear on page 52. Vicki Betts of the University of Texas at Tyler Library graciously allowed me to use her transcripts from historic newspapers. David Howard provided the photograph of William Henry Webb, a soldier from the 31st Texas Cavalry. Garrett Lewis spent a day in the field with me, walking the battlefields at Massard Prairie and Devil's Backbone. Justin Douglas helped pinpoint artifact recovery locations at Massard Prairie and spent an afternoon discussing the battle and establishment of the battlefield park with me. Pollard

Hickman Coates IV (aka "Fourth") provided the Tolliver letter used herein. Thank you all for your assistance.

Thank you also to my many friends in history in Arkansas, Oklahoma, Texas and Kansas for encouraging and supporting this effort. When the manuscript was finished during the winter of 2006-2007, I had doubts as to whether it would ever be published. Illness has a way of sapping a person's energy and motivation. Incredible support from friends and family made the difference and the book is finished.

Dale Cox

"...Although I will not pretend to say,
as some newspaper writers do, that it
'was the bloodiest battle of the war,'
yet it was a right gallant little affair."

Houston **Telegraph**
August 16, 1864

The Battle of Massard Prairie

The 1864 Confederate Attacks on Fort Smith

Chapter One

Fort Smith, Arkansas

Located at the far western edge of what once was the American frontier, Fort Smith likes to call itself the place where the "Old South meets the Old West." It is an appropriate description. Even today, this charming and picturesque city possesses a culture unlike that of any other in the nation. This was the where the real "Old West" began. Fort Smith was the gateway to a land of gunfighters, outlaws, the "Hanging Judge" and his deputy marshals. U.S. District Judge Isaac C. Parker presided at Fort Smith during the years after the Civil War and was one of the men responsible for bringing law and order to a wild frontier. He ordered the executions of more outlaws than any Federal judge in American history. Eighty-six men met their fates on the gallows at Fort Smith. It is seldom remembered, however, that 65 of his deputy marshals died in the line of duty bringing these outlaws to justice. The well-known character Rooster Cogburn, portrayed by John Wayne in the film adaptation of the book *True Grit*, may have based on a real-life one-eyed deputy marshal from Fort Smith.

Before Judge Parker and his men brought law and order to the frontier, Fort Smith was a critical point in the military history of the United States. Settled by the French during the 1700s as the community of Belle Point, the bluff and point of land at the confluence of the Arkansas and Poteau Rivers was a thriving community long before the arrival of the U.S. Army. The "privateer" Jean Laffite visited Belle Point in the years after the Battle of New Orleans and described it as a bustling little French community of several hundred residents. Names applied to area landmarks by these early hunters and trappers are still in use today: Poteau, Massard, Magazine, Petit Jean and, of course, Aux Arc (Ozark).

1

The Battle of Massard Prairie

Even before the Trail of Tears, families and groups of Cherokee began making their way into western Arkansas and eastern Oklahoma. They were under pressure from whites back east and decided to try to make new lives for themselves on new lands west of the Mississippi. Their arrival soon placed pressure on the available resources of the region and a confrontation grew between the new Cherokee settlers and the Osage, who had hunted the area for generations. As these tensions escalated, the government of the United States sent Major Stephen Long and a detachment of troops to build a new fort in hopes that a military presence might calm the situation. Long and his men arrived by boat in 1819 and constructed a log stockade atop the bluff at Belle Point. In 1822 the new outpost, Fort Smith, was reinforced by the hundreds of soldiers from Fort Scott, Georgia. The French settlement had largely disappeared.

Over the decades that followed, Fort Smith played a critical role in the history of the American frontier. The fort was an end-point for several routes of the Trail of Tears and thousands of Cherokee, Choctaw, Chickasaw, Creek and Seminole passed through. The new Choctaw and Cherokee lands were directly across the Arkansas and Poteau Rivers from the fort, so the post served as an important supply source for these Nations.

The military eventually pushed westward, building new forts and camps. Fort Smith's importance as a frontier defensive point rapidly diminished and it evolved into an important supply post. In 1838, the government started building a new, much more elaborate post at the site. With brick and stone buildings and a massive stone wall, the second Fort Smith was an elegant affair, especially when compared to the earlier log structure built by Major Long and his men. Two of the buildings of this fort still stand today and the National Park Service has marked the outlines of the other structures. Among the commanding officers of the second fort was future President Zachary Taylor, who opted not to live within the walls but built a log cabin for himself on the ridge overlooking the fort. The presumed chimney of his home can still be seen on the grounds of the Immaculate Conception Church.

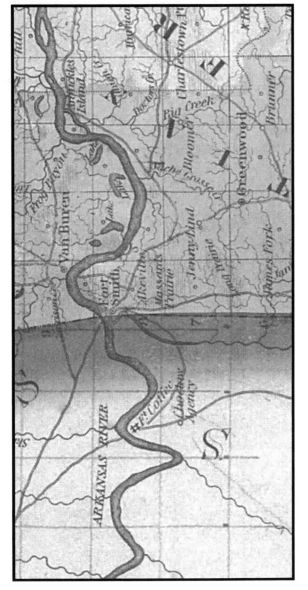

Greater Fort Smith Area, 1861–1865

This U.S. military map from the Civil War provides a reasonably accurate representation of the area around Fort Smith at the time of the Battle of Massard Prairie.
(National Park Service Collection)

The Battle of Massard Prairie

Fort Smith was an important supply and jumping off point during the war with Mexico and people across the United States knew of its existence and strategic importance. The massive fortifications planned for the site, however, were never completed. As the army pushed west, the danger of an attack on Fort Smith virtually disappeared and other than the wall itself, most of the defensive works were never constructed. A war between North and South, of course, was little contemplated at the time.

In 1849, Fort Smith became an important departure point for miners making their way to California during the Gold Rush. While many passed through on their way west to find riches, others followed in hopes of making a profit by driving livestock across the continent to sell to the miners.

A community grew up next to the fort and its businessmen were often at odds with its commanders. Merchants in the town of Fort Smith provided goods and services to both white and Native American settlers. To the chagrin of many of the officers, however, they also sold liquor to enlisted men. The community developed a reputation as a rough and tumble sort of place.

By the eve of the Civil War in 1860, the Fort Smith area presented a unique cross-section of cultures and lifestyles. Many of the Cherokee, Choctaw, Creek, Seminole and Chickasaw that had been driven west on the Trail of Tears overcame their circumstances and successfully built new lives for themselves in the Indian Territory. In fact, numerous accounts indicate that although poverty was still wide-spread in the region, many of the Native American residents in what is now Oklahoma were living better than their white counterparts across the line in western Arkansas. One visitor described them as far more "civilized" than the supposedly civilized whites.

By 1860, the population of Sebastian County was 9,238 people. Roughly 1,530 of these lived in Fort Smith. While the number is small when compared to today's population, the community was never the less one of the largest in the state. The capital of Little Rock then had a population of only around 4,000. Neighboring Crawford County, then as now closely connected to Fort Smith economically and otherwise, was home to an additional 7,850 people. Thousands more lived across the line in the Choctaw and Cherokee Nations. Scullyville, an important community near modern day Spiro, Oklahoma, had a population of between 500 and 1000.[1]

This was not the stereotypical South of *Gone with the Wind*. Arkansas had large plantations and a significant slave population, but these were largely concentrated in the Delta region in the eastern part of the state. Sebastian County was primarily an area of small farms and mountain wilderness. Of the 650 farms in the county in 1860, nearly 500 included less than 50 acres. Only 121 of the 9,238 white inhabitants held slaves and the total population of enslaved laborers in the county was 650, of all ages.[2]

Neighboring Crawford County to the north was much the same, although its farms were slightly larger. That county's 153 slaveholders (of a total population of 7,850) held 858 slaves.[3]

These numbers are extremely small when compared to the plantation districts of the state and reflect the different culture of those living on the frontier. In both the western counties of Arkansas and in the neighboring Cherokee and Choctaw Nations, most of the people worked for themselves on small farms. Those who didn't lived in communities like Fort Smith, Van Buren and Scullyville, where they worked as merchants or in a variety of other trades. There were very few manufacturing facilities of any type. Sebastian and Crawford Counties combined reported only fifteen, most of them small, a far cry from today's important industrial complex.[4]

Curiously, the residents of Sebastian and Crawford Counties were much less likely to attend church than their neighbors in other parts of the state. The two counties had a total of 27 churches with combined memberships of 3,690. Nearby Benton County, by way of comparison, was roughly the same size as Sebastian, but census takers identified 40 churches there with combined congregations of 10,350. The latter number was actually higher than the population of the county, probably a reflection of its location on the Missouri border. The

---

[1] U.S. Census for Sebastian and Crawford Counties, Arkansas, 1860; Scullyville population estimated from 1880 Census of the Choctaw Nation.
[2] U.S. Census for Sebastian County, Arkansas, 1860.
[3] U.S. Census for Crawford County, Arkansas, 1860.
[4] U.S. Census for Sebastian and Crawford Counties, Arkansas, 1860.

residents of Benton County were five times more likely to attend church than those of Sebastian County, an interesting statistic that may confirm Fort Smith's legendary reputation as a rough and rowdy frontier town.[5]

The economy of the community depended heavily on the military and the garrison, in turn, depended heavily on supplies brought up the Arkansas River. Even before Arkansas seceded from the Union, authorities in Little Rock began to contemplate the seizure of Fort Smith. On February 8, 1861, they took control of the Little Rock Arsenal and at about the same time interdicted a shipment of ordnance supplies and other stores moving upriver to Fort Smith. The seizure included 130,000 cartridges, cavalry saddles and other necessities for the garrison and its dependent posts to the west.

The situation became much more critical in April when the state once again intercepted vessels bound up the Arkansas River to Fort Smith. The seizure this time included the fort's annual shipment of supplies. Captain W.S. Burns went down to Pine Bluff to try to negotiate the situation, but was alarmed by what he found:

> ...I very soon discovered that the revolution was general. Troops were enrolling to march on Fort Smith. The steamboat I came down on was chartered. When I arrived at Pine Bluff, I found the *Silver Lake, No. 2,* tied up and strongly guarded. The crew had left, the stores placed in different houses in town, and the steamboat was to transport troops to Fort Smith.
>
> I learned from Mr. Bell, the agent (I believe) of the governor, that he had instructions to cause the stores to be sent to Little Rock, part of them to be used in the expedition to Fort Smith, for which 5,000 troops were called out.

He recommended to superiors that future supply shipments be sent via Kansas and warned of the coming attack.

---

[5] *Ibid.*; U.S. Census for Benton County, Arkansas, 1860.

Chapter One

The news that 5,000 militia were being assembled for an assault on Fort Smith was a shock to Captain Samuel D. Sturgis, the temporary commandant of the fort and a future Union general. His total force consisted of only a few companies of cavalry and some supply officers. The defenses of the fort had never been completed and Sturgis knew that he had little if any chance of holding the works against a determined assault by thousands of Arkansans. He loaded twenty wagons with all the supplies he could move and evacuated the post at 9 p.m. on the night of April 23, 1861. Behind he left the steward, chief bugler, a few sick and hospitalized soldiers and the laundresses, all under the command of Captain Alexander Montgomery, Assistant Quartermaster:

> *The causes which induced me to evacuate the post I presume are known to the department commander from general notoriety. After the supplies were cut off by the State of Arkansas the post, of course, became untenable, and we could have occupied it in any case but a few more days. One hour after we left, two boats arrived with three hundred men and ten pieces of artillery. To have contended against this force with two companies of cavalry, and that, too, while the entire population of the surrounding county were ready at a moment's warning to take up arms against us, could only resulted eventually in our being taken prisoners and the loss to the Government of all the arms, horses, means of transportation, &c., at the post.[6]*

The state troops reached Fort Smith two hours after the departure of Sturgis and his men. Consisting of 235 men with a battery of artillery instead of the 5,000 promised by state authorities, they were led by Colonel Solon Borland, an aide-de-camp to the governor. The fort was promptly seized, Montgomery and the other soldiers taken as prisoners of war, the government supplies and other property still

---

[6] Maj. Samuel D. Sturgis, Report of May 21, 1861, *Official Records*, Series 1, Volume 1, pp. 650-651.

housed there declared possessions of the state. Major Richard C. Gatlin of the 5th U.S. Infantry was visiting the fort at the time and was also taken prisoner, but later swore allegiance to the Confederacy and served as a general in North Carolina.[7]

For the next two years, Fort Smith remained a Confederate headquarters. Thousands of troops gathered there and in neighboring Van Buren prior to the 1862 Pea Ridge and Prairie Grove campaigns. Despite the strategic victories achieved by the Federals in both battles, they did not seriously threaten the fort until late December of 1862 when the Union army marched over the Boston Mountains and captured Van Buren. While this force inflicted considerable damage and sent Confederate troops scrambling to safety, the Union commanders were not prepared to maintain a presence on the Arkansas River and withdrew back across the mountains to Northwest Arkansas within a few days.

It was not until the late summer of the next year that Fort Smith itself came under attack. Major General James G. Blunt and the Army of the Frontier advanced down through the Indian Territory in August of 1863, driving the Confederate troops of Brigadier General W.L. Cabell ahead of them. By the night of August 31, 1863, Cabell was in position just west of the Poteau River about nine miles from Fort Smith. The Federals expected a severe battle the next day, but Cabell decided he had no chance of winning:

> *Knowing positively that the enemy had at least 2,300 effective men and eight pieces of artillery, and knowing that I could rely on but little more than one-half of the small number of men I had to fight, I determined to fall back, and to reach, if possible, a range of mountains in my rear, and to get all the trains and public property of every description across these mountains, with the hope that I might possibly save them.*[8]

---

[7] Capt. Alexander Montgomery, Report of April 24, 1861, *Ibid.*, p. 651.
[8] Brig. Gen. W.L. Cabell, Report of December 7, 1863, *Official Records*, Series 1, Volume 22, Part One, pp. 606-607.

Chapter One

When the Union troops advanced the next morning, they found Cabell in full retreat. His wagon trains had been ordered to the town of Waldron in Scott County via the small community of Jenny Lind southeast of Fort Smith. The general followed behind with his deteriorating army, trying to protecting the supply wagons as they moved south and across the Devil's Backbone, an east-west mountain ridge that stretches across the horizon south of Fort Smith.

The Confederate rear guard clashed with pursuing Federals at Jenny Lind at around 9 a.m. on the 1st, pulling back ahead of them and drawing them on to an ambush that Cabell had prepared at the Devil's Backbone. The Union cavalry rode headlong into the trap:

> *At 12 o'clock we came to their rear guard in ambush, whose deadly fire cut down Captain Lines and 10 or 12 of his command. I found a line of dismounted cavalry and howitzers and steadily drove their rear from their position, and up the mountain side, to within one-fourth of a mile of their line of battle, skillfully formed upon the summit of Backbone Mountain of the Poteau range. I here brought my whole force into action, and for three hours the battle raged with variable violence.[9]*

After a determined stand behind rock breastworks atop the mountain near present-day Greenwood, the Confederate force suddenly broke and ran. Cabell's dream of mauling the Federals on the mountain slope and driving them back ended in a whimper:

> *There was nothing to make these regiments run, except the sound of the cannon. Had they fought as troops fighting for liberty should, I would have captured the whole of the enemy's command, and gone back to Fort Smith, and driven the remainder of the enemy's*

[9] Col. William F. Cloud, Report of September 20, 1863, *Official Records*, Series 1, Volume 22, Part One, pp. 602-603.

force off, and retaken the place. As it was, I was forced, on account of the smallness of my force, to content myself with repulsing the enemy and protecting the public property.[10]

The Confederate defeat at the Battle of Devil's Backbone ended forever the Southern government's control of Fort Smith. While Cabell and Colonel William F. Cloud were fighting at the Backbone, General Blunt and the rest of his army had occupied the fort. Hundreds of Cabell's men deserted following the battle and many of them promptly joined the Union force. As many as three officers and 100 men who had fought against the Federals at Devil's Backbone fought beside them eight days later at Dardanelle, many still wearing their Confederate uniforms.

Union troops quickly consolidated their position at Fort Smith. Hundreds of Southern sympathizers fled the area, including most of the slaveholders and their human property. The region around the town turned into a "no man's land" patrolled by irregular bands of Southern bushwhackers who struck at Unionist homes and ambushed Federal soldiers whenever possible. The war entered a bloody and brutal phase and the civilian population suffered as it never had before.

---

[10] Cabell, December 7, 1863.

A. **The confluence of the Arkansas and Poteau Rivers.**

B. **Historic Barracks Building at Fort Smith.**

C. Quartermaster's Storehouse at Fort Smith.

D. Interior of the Quartermaster's Storehouse.

Chapter Two

Preliminary Episodes

Once they had possession of Fort Smith, Union commanders quickly turned their attention to holding it. The task was complicated by a strange command alignment that placed the town of Fort Smith and the surrounding area in the Department of Arkansas while the actual fort and neighboring Indian Territory were in the Department of Kansas. This meant that the commanding officer of the military post of Fort Smith had no authority over soldiers or civilians in the town, while the troops guarding the town were unable to draw supplies, munitions or other necessities from the storehouses of the fort.[11]

As can be imagined, this resulted in a turf battle that led to a flood of reports, letters, orders and counter-orders reaching all the way to Washington, D.C. Fortunately, the troops of the fort and the troops of the town cooperated well enough to begin the construction of a series of additional fortifications around Fort Smith.

Work on the first of these started in February of 1864 when General Samuel Curtis, the commander of the Department of Kansas, inspected Fort Smith and ordered the construction of three earthen redoubts on hilltops commanding the approaches to the main fort. He instructed officers at the fort to requisition heavy artillery and recommended a significant strengthening of their defenses.[12]

Two of the new earthworks were built on the hilltops overlooking the Van Buren and Texas Road approaches to the town, while the third

---

[11] For a good account of this unusual situation, please see Edwin C. Bearss and Arrell M. Gibson, *Fort Smith: Little Gibraltar on the Arkansas*, University of Oklahoma Press, 1979, pp. 270-278.

[12] Gen. Samuel Curtis to Gen. H.W. Halleck, February 10, 1864, *Official Records*, Series 1, Volume 34, Part Two, pp. 292-293.

stood on the hill adjacent to today's Immaculate Conception Catholic Church. The soldiers working on the earthworks suffered from hunger and unpredictable weather. Provisions were short and temperatures ranged from bitter cold to unseasonably warm, the changes often foreshadowed by heavy rain. Despite such problems, the fortifications slowly took shape.[13]

The work slowed in March when most of the soldiers from Fort Smith marched out to take part in the ill-fated Arkansas phase of the Red River Campaign. Local civilians stepped forward to continue the project, their efforts spurred on by reports that a Confederate expedition was marching north to recapture Fort Smith. Four significant earthwork forts were eventually completed and a line of rifle pits stretched from the Poteau River in a loop around the town to the Arkansas River. The trenches enclosed the entire community and connected the forts. Each of the redoubts was armed with two 12-pounders and additional artillery was placed in the main fort as well. The work crews further strengthened the main by piling earth against its stone walls.

The regular soldiers returned from the Red River Campaign in May, having learned at Poison Spring and Jenkins Ferry that the Confederates could and would fight for Arkansas. They now joined in the completion of the fortifications with renewed vigor. Once the two mile long line of entrenchments was completed, fields of fire were cleared and lines of abatis or entanglements placed outside the works to help slow down an infantry assault.

The Confederates, meanwhile, took advantage of the opportunity provided to them by the successful outcome of the Red River Campaign and launched a determined effort to retake much of Arkansas and the Indian Territory. General Samuel B. Maxey sent Brigadier General Douglas H. Cooper's cavalry to push north into Indian Territory. By June Southern soldiers were again ranging freely to the outskirts of Fort Smith. Making matters worse for the Federals, bands of Confederate raiders and guerillas swarmed the Boston Mountains

---

[13] Tom Wing, Ed., "A Rough Introduction to This Sunny Land": The Civil War Diary of Private Henry A. Strong, Co. K, Twelfth Kansas Infantry, Butler Center for Arkansas Studies, Central Arkansas Library System, 2006, pp. 17-32 (hereafter Strong, Diary).

north of town, intercepting traffic on the Telegraph Road to Fayetteville, cutting telegraph lines and otherwise wreaking havoc.

In mid-April, the Confederates attacked three Union companies assigned to guard a supply of cotton at Roseville, a small community on the river near Fort Smith. Although they were unable to overrun the outpost, the raiders burned 133 bales of cotton and inflicted casualties. A surgeon from Fort Smith set out with a cavalry escort of 25 men to tend to the wounded, but was ambushed himself about ten miles west of Roseville. Assistant Surgeon Stephen Fairchild and eleven members of his escort were killed.

Then in mid-June, Colonel Stand Watie, the famed Cherokee Confederate leader, attacked the steamboat *J.R. Williams* as it headed upstream from Fort Smith with a shipment of supplies for Fort Blunt (Gibson). Disabling the boat with artillery fire, Watie captured it, looted the supplies and burned the vessel to the waterline.

Confederate scouts and guerillas also hovered around Fort Smith itself, reporting on troop dispositions and firing into the Union lines from time to time.

The early summer of 1864 was more rainy than normal and rivers and creeks in the area overflowed their banks. Private Henry Strong of the 12th Kansas Infantry watched the Arkansas River rise 10 feet in two days and reported seeing barrels of flour and other items floating downstream in the flooded river, a sure sign of Confederate raids upriver. The high water helped steamboat traffic on the river and allowed the Federals to continue bringing supplies up to Fort Smith through the normal dry season. Strong wrote, however, that it hampered efforts to pursue Confederate raiders. Swamps and creeks were full and crossings all but impossible.[14]

The water did not, however, slow the movements of the more versatile Confederates. General Cooper pushed up to the old Choctaw Council House near Tuskahoma, Oklahoma, about 90 miles southwest of Fort Smith. He met there with his primary subordinates, Brigadier Generals R.M. Gano of Texas and Stand Watie of the Cherokee Nation. With the possible exception of Nathan Bedford Forrest, there may not

---

[14] Strong, Diary, pp. 51-53.

have been two better men in the Confederacy for the operations planned by Cooper.

A 30-year-old doctor at the beginning of the war, Gano was a Kentuckian who moved to Texas in the 1850s after practicing medicine for a couple of years in Baton Rouge, Louisiana. He settled on Grapevine Prairie, where the Dallas-Fort Worth International Airport stands today, where he raised stock, farmed and practiced medicine. He was also involved in a guerilla war with Comanche raiding parties and served in the state legislature. When Texas seceded, he raised two companies of cavalry and headed east to join the fight. Assigned to the command of the famed Confederate raider General John Hunt Morgan, Gano served in all of Morgan's major expeditions and fought in numerous engagements. By January of 1863, he was a colonel commanding the First Brigade of Morgan's Division and in September he fought at Chickamauga under Nathan Bedford Forrest.

Promoted to the rank of brigadier general, Gano returned west in October of 1863 with the 80 survivors of his original squadron (now called the "Gano Guards"). Given command of the Texas cavalry in the Trans-Mississippi Department, he helped turn back the Union's Red River Campaign and was wounded in the arm during the fighting in Arkansas. By the summer of 1864, however, he had turned 34-years old and was in the Choctaw Nation, spoiling for a fight.

Stand Watie, of course, was the only Native American to achieve the rank of a general officer in the service of the Confederacy. Born near Rome, Georgia, in 1806, he was 58-years-old during the summer of 1864. A tough intellectual who sometimes wrote for the *Cherokee Phoenix*, he had believed that the Cherokee would eventually be forced from their homes in the East, so he voluntarily relocated to what is now Oklahoma prior to the Trail of Tears. Following the military removal of the rest of the nation, he survived assassination attempts by the anti-removal Ross Party. Despite such animosity, he served in the Cherokee Council for nearly 20 years and developed a successful plantation, farming his lands through the use of slave laborers.

An ardent supporter of the Confederate cause, Watie became the colonel of the 1st Cherokee Mounted Rifles in 1861. He took part in numerous raids and engagements in Indian Territory as the war quickly turned into a blood-letting due to the divided nature of loyalties in the region. In March of 1862 he fought at the Battle of Pea Ridge, Arkansas, where his men overran a Union artillery position and were accused of scalping and otherwise mutilating fatally wounded Union soldiers.

Watie served in a diversionary role during the Prairie Grove Campaign, but fought again fought at the Battle of Elk Creek or Honey Springs in 1863. Even after Union troops occupied most of the Cherokee Nation, he remained loyal to the Confederacy and continued to fight and raid. General Maxey promoted him to brigadier general in 1864 and assigned him to Cooper's command.

Douglas H. Cooper was 48 years old during the summer of 1864. A native of Mississippi, he had studied at the University of Virginia with future Confederate Generals Lafayette McLaws and "Prince" John Magruder. He was farming and serving in the Mississippi State Legislature when the Mexican-American War erupted in 1846. Like many of his fellow citizens he volunteered for service and became a captain in the Mississippi Rifles, a regiment commanded by future Confederate President Jefferson Davis. Cooper fought in the Battles of Monterey and Buena Vista and was cited for gallantry and courage under fire.

After the war, with help from Davis, he obtained an appointment as U.S. Agent to the Choctaw and relocated to the Indian Territory. Noted for his fair treatment of the Native Americans, he became widely respected by them. When the Civil War erupted in 1861, Cooper raised the 1st Choctaw and Chickasaw Mounted Rifles and became the colonel of the Native American unit. He fought at the Battles of Round Mountain, Chustenahlah, Pea Ridge and Newtonia and was promoted to brigadier general in 1863. Surprised and soundly defeated a short time later at the Battle of Elk Creek (Honey Springs) he fell back and took part in the Red River Campaign. But by the summer of 1864, General Cooper was back in the Choctaw Nation.

Making solid use of his cavalry, both white and Native American, Cooper probed and harassed the Federals at Fort Smith. As a result, solid intelligence began flowing back to his headquarters.

The Battle of Massard Prairie

The Union troops at Fort Smith knew they were being watched, but seem to have been somewhat oblivious to the immediacy of the danger. On July 26, 1864, just one day before the Battle of Massard Prairie, a soldier identifying himself only as "Amigo" wrote from Fort Smith to the Leavenworth, Kansas, *Daily Times*, that a large Confederate force was hovering nearby:

> *To the superficial observer military matters seem quiet here just now, though it is generally understood that the rebels have a considerable force south of this place. Whether they intend an attack here, or simply draw our attention while they strike at some other point, or a raid on a grand scale, may not be developed for a few weeks; that they are active no one doubts.*
>
> *There is very little forage being secured at this place, though a contract for furnishing several hundred tons has been let. There will not be grain sufficient to supply the domestic wants and our mules and horses, for two months, raised in reach of this place, though the military authorities promised the citizens all the protection necessary to enable them to live in peace at home and cultivate their farms.*[15]

Despite the promises of military protection, few of the local civilians were foolish enough to try to farm with Confederate raiders and irregular guerillas roaming at will. Most of the largest farms in the area were completely abandoned and the lack of forage for military animals reached critical levels.

To save as many of the horses and mules as possible, Brigadier General John Thayer, now in command of the finally unified troops at Fort Smith, sent out large detachments of troops to guard hay cutting parties and protect herds sent to graze on the surrounding prairies. One of these detachments camped at Flat Rock Creek in Indian

---

[15]"Letter from Fort Smith", July 26, 1864, published in the Leavenworth, Kansas, *Daily Times*, August 7, 1864.

Chapter Two

Territory, another at Caldwell's Place on the Jenny Lind Road south of Fort Smith and a third at the Picnic Grove on Massard Prairie.

Thayer was risking disaster by putting so many men in exposed positions, but the desperate need for forage gave him little choice. The Confederates now had the opportunity they had been watching and waiting for and they wasted little time in exploiting it.

E. Reconstructed Wall Section at Fort Smith National Historic Site.

F. Cannon and reconstructed post Civil War gallows at Fort Smith.

Chapter Three

Planning the Attack

At his headquarters near the old Choctaw Council House, General Cooper considered his options. His troops had struck hard both above and below the fort, but the general knew that an attempt to storm the now completed outer works would be costly at best, disastrous at worst. Without siege artillery and with a force that consisted mostly of cavalry, he doubted the wisdom of trying to assault Fort Smith by force.

At the beginning of the last week of July 1864, however, Cooper's reconnaissance parties brought in news that detachments of Union cavalry were camped in exposed positions at Caldwell's place on the Jenny Lind Road and in the Picnic Grove on Massard Prairie. Since the former group was believed to consist of Unionist cavalry from Arkansas, or "Arkansas Feds" as the Confederates called them, Cooper decided to move against them first. This camp was also believed to be the most exposed of the two:

> *...On the 26ᵗʰ of July General Gano was directed to have a detachment of 500 men from his brigade ready by 3 p.m. for a scout. Detachments from the Second Indian Brigade, under Col. S.N. Folsom, and from Wells' battalion, under Lieutenant-Colonel Wells, were also ordered to be in readiness. Lieut. Col. Jack McCurtain was directed to take post with his Choctaw battalion by sunrise next morning on the Devil's Backbone. Capt. J. Henry Minhart was instructed to report to the senior officer present with the detachments as a guide to conduct the expedition; the*

whole, except McCurtain's battalion, to rendezvous on
Poteau, near Page's Ferry, by dark.[16]

The men selected for the attack were some of the hardest fighting mounted troops in the service of the Confederacy. The men of Gano's brigade, including his own elite "Gano Guards," were hard riding Texans with considerable battle experience. They came from the 1st and 5th Texas Partisan Rangers and the 29th Texas Cavalry. The 1st and 5th Partisan Rangers were also known as the 30th and 31st Texas Cavalries. The entire strength of these units did not take part in the raid. According to Cooper, around 500 men were detached under Gano for the attack.

Colonel S.N. Folsom's men were Choctaw and Chickasaw warriors. Most had been riding for the Confederacy since the beginning of the war as the 2nd Choctaw Cavalry. They were experienced and daring soldiers that had fought in a number of engagements in both Arkansas and the Indian Territory.

Lieutenant Colonel John W. Wells was the commander of a battalion of six companies of Texas cavalry. Primarily enlisted in the areas of northern Texas that bordered the Choctaw Nation, many of these men had fought at Prairie Grove, Dripping Springs, Van Buren, Elk Creek (Honey Springs) and Perryville.

Finally, Lieutenant Colonel Jack McCurtain's men formed a battalion of mounted rifles that would become the 3rd Choctaw Cavalry by the end of the war. Like the other Confederates, they were seasoned soldiers and excellent horsemen, with considerable battlefield experience.

The exact size of the force ordered to assemble for the raid is not known. The Federals estimated Gano's command at 2,000 men, but this is a clear exaggeration. Including McCurtain's force, which remained in position at Devil's Backbone, the total command probably numbered around 1,000 men. One Southern participant estimated the

---

[16] Brig. Gen. Douglas H. Cooper, Report of August 10, 1864, *Official Records*, Series 1, Volume 41, Part One, p. 31.

number actually on the battlefield at between 600 and 800. Other estimates were similar.[17]

Brave and determined, they were short on supplies and poorly armed. Captain J.J. DuBose, Cooper's chief ordnance officer, provided some enlightenment to the state of the arming of Cooper's men when he wrote that Folsom's, Wells' and McCurtain's soldiers were armed with a few Enfield rifles, a "very, very few Mississippi rifles," double-barrel guns, Texas rifles, sporting rifles and pretty much any other firearm they could lay their hands on:

> *A regiment armed complete with these guns are armed but badly. These guns are nothing more than a cheat, badly put together and very unreliable, being liable, a great number, to burst....Lieutenant Colonel Wells' battalion were armed with Texas rifles, double-barrel shotguns, and a very few muskets with very few exceptions. I did not see a gun that was entirely serviceable.[18]*

Officers had pleaded for clothing and arms for these men. General Maxey wrote that they were "literally ragged and barefoot" and that "shirts, drawers, socks and pants are necessary for decency." Union General Thayer in Fort Smith made a similar observation, reporting that the Confederate horsemen were armed with infantry weapons but, "Their clothing is very poor and insufficient in quality." It is no wonder the troops in the Indian Territory were quick to strip dead, wounded or captured Federals of their weapons and clothing.[19]

---

[17] Capt. William Murphy Cravens to Mary Eloise Cravens, July 28, 1864, quoted by Steve Cox, "The Action on Massard Prairie," *The Journal* of the Fort Smith Historical Society, Volume 4, Number 1, April 1980, p. 11.
[18] Capt. J.J. DuBose, Report of February 1864, quoted by Frank Cunningham, *General Stand Watie's Confederate Indians*, University of Oklahoma Press (Reprint edition), 1998, p. 137.
[19] *Ibid.*, p. 138.

The Battle of Massard Prairie

Despite such shortcomings in material, most Union and Confederate commanders agreed that the men were well-disciplined, well-mounted and good fighters.[20]

Cooper's plan of attack was outlined in his "Special Orders, No. 86." The original document can no longer be found, but is summarized in the general's subsequent report on the Battle of Massard Prairie:

> *The plan...was for Col. S.N. Folsom, commanding detachment from Indian division, to attack the camp of Federal's at Caldwell's, on the Jenny Lind road, capture or destroy it if possible, and if pursued by other troops on Massard Prairie or from Fort Smith to retreat by the Fort Towson road over the Devil's Backbone, where McCurtain lay in ambush; the detachment from Gano's brigade to remain concealed near Page's, on Cedar Prairie, until the Federals should pass in pursuit of Folsom, and then attack them in rear, while Folsom and McCurtain should turn upon them at the Backbone.*[21]

The landmarks described by Cooper were well-known in 1864, but for the most part have vanished from the landscape of today. Devil's Backbone, of course, still exists and stretches from east to west across the horizon south of Fort Smith. The Fort Towson road, today's Towson Avenue, was so named because it ran from Fort Smith down through the Choctaw Nation to Fort Towson on the Red River. One of the primary routes in and out of Fort Smith, it remains today one of the city's major traffic arteries. From the point where the modern four-lane curves to become Zero Street, the original road (as does Highway 271) continued south over the first mountain (partially occupied to the east by today's Fianna Hills subdivision) and on to the Devil's Backbone. After crossing the ridge, it curved southwest into Oklahoma and crossed the Poteau River. The modern communities of Bonanza and Hackett are along this route. To the east of this road as it left Fort

---

[20] *Ibid.*
[21] Cooper, 1864, p. 31.

24

Smith, now largely covered by industrial and residential areas, was Massard Prairie. To the southwest was Cedar Prairie where Gano was instructed to wait with his men for a chance to strike the pursuing Federal troops from behind.

It was a well conceived plan. By showing only a small portion of their strike force, Cooper and Gano knew there was a reasonable chance the Union cavalry would come out of Fort Smith in pursuit. With McCurtain's Choctaws in a blocking position on the Backbone, Gano could sweep in behind the Federals with the main body of the Confederate force and close the trap. It was an old strategy, dating back thousands of years, but an effective one that is still studied and used by military forces today.

The operation began on the afternoon of July 26, 1864. Moving across the border from the Choctaw Nation, McCurtain's men took up positions atop the crest of the Devil's Backbone at the point where the Fort Towson Road crossed the mountain. Along most of this mountain, the rock formations at the top create natural breastworks that look almost like manmade fortifications. Confederate troops had earlier used similar formations to the east during the Battle of Devil's Backbone. By piling a few extra rocks into the gaps in the natural spine of the mountain, McCurtain's soldiers would be able to hold back a much larger force.

Gano proceeded to Page's Ferry on the Poteau where he expected to rendezvous with the other troops by dark. When they arrived, however, he was disappointed. The units under Folsom and Wells were smaller than expected. Reassessing the situation instead of blindly following orders, Gano decided that he did not have enough men to carry out the operation as originally planned.[22]

Instead of dividing his force into three separate units, the general decided to significantly change the design of the operation. While McCurtain was left in his position on the Backbone, Gano combined the rest of the force into a single column. To better utilize this force, the general decided to go forward in person with the main body instead of lurking in an ambush position on Cedar Prairie. Considering this

---

[22] *Ibid.*

change in the alignment of his force, Gano decided that the Union camp on Massard Prairie offered a much more inviting target. By striking at dawn and bringing a larger command into the fight, he hoped to overrun the Federals before they could put up much resistance. If the fight proved too much for him, he would still be able to fall back to the Devil's Backbone and rely on assistance from Lieutenant Colonel McCurtain's men.[23]

The Confederates began their approach as night fell across the borderlands. The way that had seemed so clear in broad daylight suddenly became confusing in the dark of night:

> ...Through the incompetency of our guides and the multiplicity of Indian trails, the brigade got lost. We blundered about until midnight, finally found the road, crossed the Poteau river, and marched to within four miles, as our guides informed us, of the position of the enemy. It was the intention of Gen. Gano to attack them at daylight.[24]

Stumbling around in the dark in search of the right road proved time consuming and exhausting. By the time Gano had his men at the point his guides told him was the right position, the Southern troops had only about two hours to rest before they had to be back up and in their saddles Finally assured that they were in the right spot, the cavalrymen fell from their horses and slept on the ground as best they could. They thought they were only about two miles from their target.[25]

The Union troops at Massard Prairie consisted of a battalion of four companies from the 6th Kansas Cavalry under the command of Captain (acting major) David Mefford. They had occupied a semi-permanent camp there since their return from the Red River Campaign.

---

[23] *Ibid.*
[24] "The Fight at Diamond Grove, Arkansas," written on July 28, 1864 in "Camp 20 miles south of Fort Smith,' published in the *Galveston Weekly News*, August 17, 1864, p. 2, transcribed by Vicki Betts.
[25] *Ibid.*

26

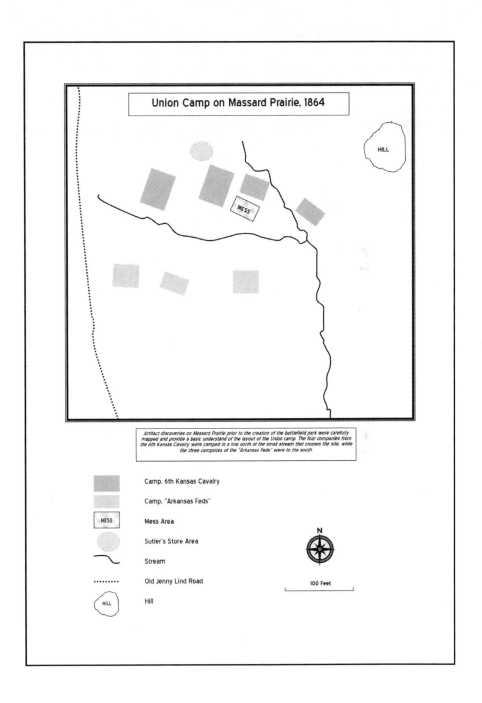

Union Camp on Massard Prairie, 1864

HILL

MESS

Artifact discoveries on Massard Prairie prior to the creation of the battlefield park were carefully mapped and provide a basic understand of the layout of the Union camp. The four companies from the 6th Kansas Cavalry were camped in a line north of the small stream that crosses the site, while the three campsites of the "Arkansas Feds" were to the south.

Camp, 6th Kansas Cavalry

Camp, "Arkansas Feds"

Mess Area

Sutler's Store Area

Stream

Old Jenny Lind Road

Hill

N

100 Feet

G. Devil's Backbone near the planned Ambush Site.

H. Site of the Camp of the 6th Kansas Cavalry.

Chapter Three

The tents of the encampment were grouped by company in what locals called the Picnic or "Round" Grove. This grove of trees grew along a slight rise overlooking the north bank of a tiny stream that trickled across the prairie. To improve their supply of water for drinking and cooking, the soldiers placed rocks in the creek to back up the water and create a small pool.[26]

The grove of trees provided some shelter for the men from the harsh summer sun and was remembered by those who spent time there as a pleasant spot. It remains so today.

The companies were camped in roughly an east-west line through the grove, paralleling the small creek. Company B was on the western flank of this line, with Companies D, E and H stretching to the east in that order. The total length of the line of encampments was less than 500 feet. Artifact discoveries at the site by the Southwest American Historical Artifact Association (S.A.H.A.R.A.) prior to the creation of the battlefield park fortunately were mapped by the organization. When viewed in connection with the eyewitness accounts of the battle, the S.A.H.A.R.A. map makes it possible to reconstruct the action on the ground with relative ease.[27]

In addition to the four companies of the 6th Kansas Cavalry, Confederate accounts also report the presence of a number of "Arkansas Federals" at the grove. Union accounts are silent on this point, but there is reason to believe that the Southern reports were accurate.

On July 5, 1864, about three weeks before the battle, a group of 100 men wrote to the editor of Fort Smith's *New Era* newspaper from their encampment on "Mazard Prairie." They were members of the 4th Arkansas U.S. Infantry and wrote to express their loyalty to the Union despite the desertion of a number of men from their unit. The letter pointed out that many of the original recruits of their unit had deserted because they were detested by the "Union boys" and because their families were exposed to raids by bushwhackers. Those who remained

---

[26] This use of the creek was verified by experts from Vicksburg National Military Park who examined the battlefield. These stones can still be seen, although the stream itself is usually dry.

[27] Steve Cox, "The Action at Massard Prairie," pp. 12-13.

felt they were being treated unfairly by their fellow Union soldiers and the citizens of the town alike:

> *Under these circumstances we came to lay our all on the altar of our country, many of us having competent estates. We never owned slaves, no! We never bought one, sold one, held an interest in as much as old Shylock's pound of human flesh. We come with clean hands, we are Union soldiers, and like the Romans of old, we call on the army and the community to award us the honor and distinction due to American soldiers as long as we are faithful.*[28]

The 4th Arkansas U.S. was a short-lived unit organized in Fort Smith during the winter and spring of 1864. When it was at full strength it mustered 173 men including officers and a surgeon, or the equivalent of about three companies. By the time of the July 5th letter from Massard Prairie, the strength of the unit had fallen to around 100 men, an indication that 73 had deserted, died, been discharged or for other reasons were no longer associated with the battalion. When the 4th was disbanded in October of 1864 and merged with the 2nd Arkansas U.S. Infantry, only one captain and around 75 men remained.[29]

During their mapping of artifact locations on the battlefield site in 1979, the S.A.H.A.R.A. members located the sites of three temporary camps in the woods opposite the creek from the more permanent camps of the four 6th Kansas Cavalry companies. All three camps were of company size. Since the 4th Arkansas at its largest had enough men to field about three companies of infantry and since it is known that at least 100 men from the unit were camped on Massard Prairie less than three weeks prior to the battle, it is logical to conclude that these were the men who occupied the three campsites discovered by the artifact

---

[28] "Protest" to the editor of the *New Era*, July 5, 1864, reprinted in the Little Rock *Unconditional Union*, August 4, 1864, p. 1, transcribed by Vicki Betts.
[29] Index to Compiled Military Service Records; Official Army Register of the Volunteer Force, 1861-1865.

association. It is also reasonable to conclude that they were the "Arkansas Federals" observed by the Confederate forces.[30]

The primary purpose of the camp on the prairie was to protect a large herd of horses sent out to graze on the rich grasses. The mission of the 6th Kansas Cavalry, and presumably the 4th Arkansas U.S. Infantry, was to protect this herd from raids by Confederate troops or bushwhackers. Each day the cavalrymen would move the animals out onto the open prairie where they could graze, keep watch over them, and then bring them back in closer to camp each night.

To provide some advance warning in the event of attack, Captain Mefford had ordered Sergeant Tubbs from Company D to establish a picket post on the Jenny Lind Road south of the camp. Other outlying picket posts could also be expected to provide early warning, including a rather large semi-permanent one on the Texas Road occupied by 2nd Lieutenant Levi Stewart and 35 men from Company I, 6th Kansas Cavalry. Another group of men from Company L, 6th Kansas Cavalry, was also in the open in the same general vicinity, but their exact location is not clear.[31]

From numerous letters written by soldiers serving at Fort Smith in July, there is no doubt that the troops were aware of a large Confederate force operating in the area. It is logical to assume that they would have been concerned about the possibility of attack, but apparently they were not. As night fell on July 26, 1864, the soldiers in the camp on Massard Prairie went about their normal routine and soon were slumbering the night away. They were completely unaware and evidently unconcerned about the fury that would descend on them with the first light of the next morning.

---

[30] Steve Cox, "The Action at Massard Prairie," pp. 12-13.
[31] Lt. William Burgoyne, Report of July 29, 1864, *Official Records*, Series 1, Volume 53, pp. 480-481; 1st Lt. Jacob Morehead, Report of July 29, 1864, *Official Records*, Series 1, Volume 41, Part One, p. 25.

I. Entrance to Massard Prairie Battlefield Park.

J. U.D.C. Monument at Massard Prairie.

K. 6th Kansas Cavalry Position at Massard Prairie.

L. Surviving Remnant of Original Prairie.

The Battle of Massard Prairie

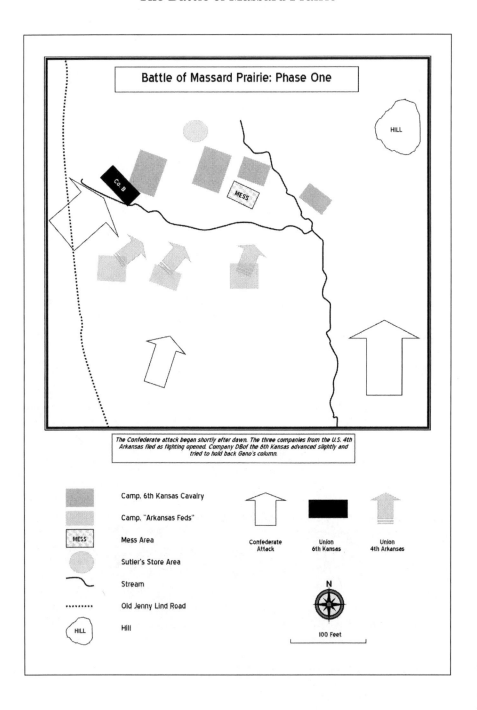

Battle of Massard Prairie: Phase One

Co. B

MESS

HILL

The Confederate attack began shortly after dawn. The three companies from the U.S. 4th Arkansas fled as fighting opened. Company D Bof the 6th Kansas advanced slightly and tried to hold back Gano's column.

Camp, 6th Kansas Cavalry

Camp, "Arkansas Feds"

MESS — Mess Area

Sutler's Store Area

Stream

Old Jenny Lind Road

HILL — Hill

Confederate Attack

Union 6th Kansas

Union 4th Arkansas

N

100 Feet

Chapter Four

The Battle of Massard Prairie

After only two hours of rest, the Confederates were back in their saddles and on the move. From the assurances of their guides, they believed they were only four miles from the Union camp. They expected to move into position on the edge of the prairie and then sweep in on the sleeping Federals at dawn. Gano quickly discovered, however, that his scouts had misjudged their position in the darkness and confusion of the previous night. Instead of being only four miles from the Union camp, his men had stopped to rest at a point more than twice that distance away.[32]

Undeterred, the general pushed his men forward. As they approached the fringe of Cedar Prairie, they ran into a group of Union pickets who were guarding the Line Road entrance to Fort Smith. The Confederates scattered them and continued moving, riding up and over the broad top of a mountain known by most area residents today as Fianna Hills. The ridge separated Cedar Prairie from Massard Prairie and as the soldiers reached the northern crest of the mountain, they could look out over the broad prairie beyond:

> *...Soon after sunrise we drove in the enemy's pickets, passed over a high mountain, and came down into Mazzard prairie, four miles from Fort Smith. At the far end of this prairie, some one and a half miles from the foot of the mountain, we discovered a beautiful island of timber, known as the Diamond or Picnic Grove, at the north end of which we spotted our game, making hasty preparations to give us a warm reception.*[33]

---

[32] *Galveston Weekly News, August 17, 1864, Page 2.*
[33] *Houston Telegraph, August 17, 1864.*

The Battle of Massard Prairie

As they rode down to the base of the mountain, Gano divided his force into two columns. The first, under Colonels Folsom and Wells, was ordered to swing around to the right and flank the enemy from the east. Gano himself would execute a similar flanking movement to the left. As his column approached the enemy, he would detach a third force to advance through the woods directly to the camp and attack the Federal center. If things went well, he hoped to surround a large number of the Union troops and force their surrender.[34]

As they moved forward across the prairie, the Confederates scattered a second post, this one on the old Jenny Lind Road. The pickets from Company D of the 6th Kansas Cavalry exchanged fire with the oncoming Confederates and fell back at a run across the prairie, shouting a warning to the rest of their unit that an attack was underway. Lieutenant William Burgoyne, the adjutant of the 6th Kansas Cavalry, was in the camp when he saw Sergeant Tubbs from Company D approaching from the southwest:

> Between 6 and 7 a.m. on the morning of the 27th instant Sergeant Tubbs, Company D, in command of picket post No. 1, on Jenny Lind road, reported to me that the enemy in force were advancing on our camp very rapidly. I immediately sent a messenger to [Colonel William R. Judson] by way of the camp of Company I, camped on the Texas road, and also sent a messenger to the commanding officer Fourteenth Kansas Cavalry, camped about two miles from us and on our left, notifying them of the approach of the enemy. Lieutenant Defriese, the officer of the day, at my suggestion started in the direction of the firing to ascertain particulars.[35]

Among the houses scattered along the southern edge of the prairie in 1864 was the home of John Barnes. About 200 yards away was another, belonging to Flem Johnson. The two families were Unionist in

---

[34] *Ibid.*
[35] Lt. William Burgoyne, Report of July 29, 1864, *Official Records.*

their sympathies and often provided food to a group of men who lived in hiding in the woods and hills south of Fort Smith. Many of these men were Confederate deserters and, to their misfortune, they had gathered at the Barnes house on the morning of July 27, 1864.

Fifteen year old James Robert Barnes, a nephew of John Barnes, was visiting with his uncle and aunt at the time of the attack:

> *One morning, they slipped into the house and my Aunt Polly fixed them some breakfast – this was just about daylight. They told me to go out on the porch and watch and see if I could see any one, and if I seen anyone, to come in and tell them. While they were getting breakfast, I saw a string of Rebels coming down the hill on the [South] side of the field. I ran to my uncle and said, "I see a bunch of Rebels coming yonder." The men made a break for the brush. Jonathan Glenn ran up the road to the West to cut into the brush and, as he did not see some of the Rebels, they got him. The others got away.[36]*

The advancing Confederates, remembered by Barnes as Choctaws, came on to the house, bringing Glenn with them. A group of them ran on to the home of Flem Johnson. Barnes remembered that, "Flem had the pneumonia and was expected by everyone to die." As the teenager watched in horror, "Rebels carried Flem out of his bed in the house and set him up against a tree and shot him to death."[37]

Things now began to happen very quickly. Less than five minutes after he had been warned that Confederates were on the prairie, Lieutenant Burgoyne of the 6th Kansas heard firing break out on the right side of the camp.[38]

---

[36] James Robert Barnes, n.d., Accounts of the original Choctaw enrollees.
[37] *Ibid.*
[38] Lt. William Burgoyne, Report of July 29, 1864, *Official Records.*

The Battle of Massard Prairie

First Lieutenant Jacob Morehead was commanding Company B that morning and his first thought was to save the herd. The horses had been moved out on the open prairie at dawn and were about three-quarters of a mile away, grazing on open ground to the southwest. Morehead sent men to retrieve them and then formed his company slightly in advance of the west end of the camp so he could protect the herd as it came in:

> ...*Before the horses could be brought up the enemy charged on us, which stampeded the herd and left the men on foot to fight as best they could. We drove the enemy back, and as I had received no orders from the commanding officer, I ordered my men to fall back until they could form on the right of the other companies. When I had fallen back to the left of my company's parade ground I came in speaking distance of Major Mefford, [from whom] I received orders to form my company on the right to protect the camp. I immediately took the position assigned me, with company D on my left. We held our position, repulsing three distinct charges of the enemy.*[39]

Artifact discoveries on the prairie prior to the creation of the battlefield park revealed a firing line just southwest of the main camp. Undoubtedly this was the point where Company B made its stand.

From his uncle's house on the edge of the prairie, James Robert Barnes could see and hear the fight as it developed at the edge of the Union camp:

> *I heard a shot, while I stood on the front porch, then a steady fire. The Federals were in bed, they came out in their night clothes, with their guns. The Rebels killed lots of Federals. I do not know how many and lots*

---

[39] Lt. Jacob Morehead, Report of July 29, 1864, *Official Records*, Series 1, Volume 41, Part One, p. 25.

of Rebels were killed, too. There was about 45 minutes of fighting there.[40]

The men of Company B opened fire as Gano's column came in range, but the Confederates pushed up on them immediately and cut off the herd. "No sooner had the head of our column come within striking distance," wrote one of the Confederates, "than the enemy opened on us with their Sharpe's rifles. It was but the work of a moment for the general to form his men, and with a Texas yell they dashed forward."[41]

Unsuccessful in his effort to save the herd, Lieutenant Morehead began to pull his troops back from their advanced position where they risked being overrun by the oncoming Confederates. Falling back to the left side of his company's parade ground, he saw Major David Mefford, commander of the camp. Mefford ordered him to form there on the right side of the camp, with Company D on his left, to try to prevent Gano from breaking through in that direction.[42]

By this point, however, the Southern general had detached a portion of his column with orders to advance through the trees and strike the Union center. The rest of his column hit the right flank and Wells and Folsom attacked the Union left. The detachment assigned to the center, all Texans under Major Carroll and Captains Welch and Hard, pushed into the grove and opened fire on the Federals from across the narrow stream.[43]

Despite the confusion, the four companies of the 6th Kansas formed a ragged line of battle along the slope between their tents and the stream. Confederate accounts indicate that the "Arkansas Federals" fled on sight, but Union reports make no mention of them. Lieutenant Burgoyne reported that just as the men started to form in response to the attack on their right, firing also opened on the left:

---

[40] James Robert Barnes, n.d.
[41] Houston *Telegraph*, August 15, 1864.
[42] Morehead, July 29, 1864.
[43] Galveston *Weekly News*, August 17, 1864.

The Battle of Massard Prairie

The men had not time to saddle. The yells of the enemy and the firing stampeded the horses. Almost all of them started across the prairie in the direction of Fort Smith. The men fell in on their company parades and moved out on the prairie with the intention of gaining the timber on the north side of the prairie, having given up all hopes of saving the camp. When the force was discovered on our left I ordered Sergeant Goss, who had about ten men mounted (of Company D), to go to the rise of ground on our left and if possible check the enemy.[44]

The Federals were now facing attack from the front, left and right and it was obvious that the Confederates were moving into their rear hoping to cut them off completely. Mefford apparently decided to withdraw his force in a fighting retreat across the prairie to the timber line and ridge to the north, a distance of a couple of miles. This decision was not communicated up and down the line, however, and the two companies on the right suddenly found themselves alone and without support:

We held our position, repulsing three distinct charges of the enemy. At this time I saw that Major Mefford had, with Companies E and H, been driven from their position on the left of the line, and had begun to fall back across the prairie. I knew that I could not hold my ground much longer with what men I had, so, without receiving orders from Major Mefford, commenced falling back toward him. As we fell back I had several men captured by the enemy that was advancing through the timber in the center of our camp.[45]

---

[44] Lt. William Burgoyne, Report of July 29, 1864, *Official Records.*
[45] Morehead, July 29, 1864

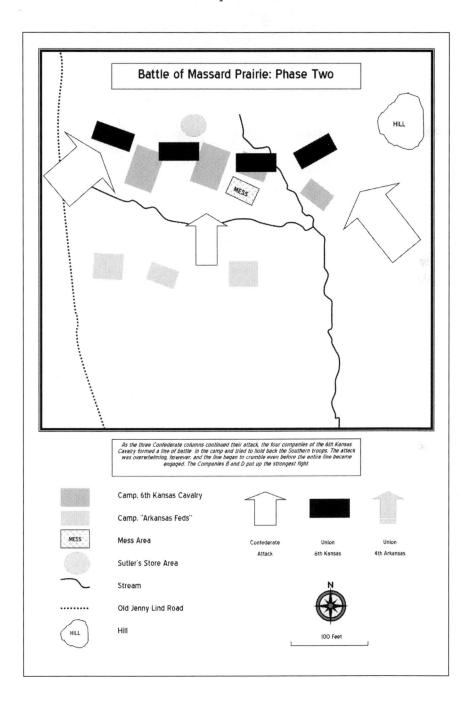

Battle of Massard Prairie: Phase Two

As the three Confederate columns continued their attack, the four companies of the 6th Kansas Cavalry formed a line of battle in the camp and tried to hold back the Southern troops. The attack was overwhelming, however, and the line began to crumble even before the entire line became engaged. The Companies B and D put up the strongest fight.

Camp, 6th Kansas Cavalry

Camp, "Arkansas Feds"

Mess Area

Sutler's Store Area

Stream

Old Jenny Lind Road

Hill

Confederate Attack

Union 6th Kansas

Union 4th Arkansas

N

100 Feet

The Battle of Massard Prairie

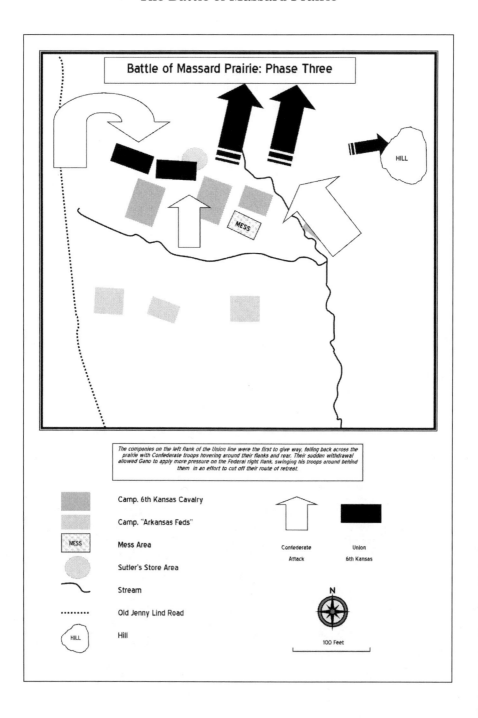

Battle of Massard Prairie: Phase Three

The companies on the left flank of the Union line were the first to give way, falling back across the prairie with Confederate troops hovering around their flanks and rear. Their sudden withdrawal allowed Gano to apply more pressure on the Federal right flank, swinging his troops around behind them in an effort to cut off their route of retreat.

Camp. 6th Kansas Cavalry

Camp. "Arkansas Feds"

MESS — Mess Area

Sutler's Store Area

Stream

Old Jenny Lind Road

HILL — Hill

Confederate Attack

Union 6th Kansas

N

100 Feet

Chapter Four

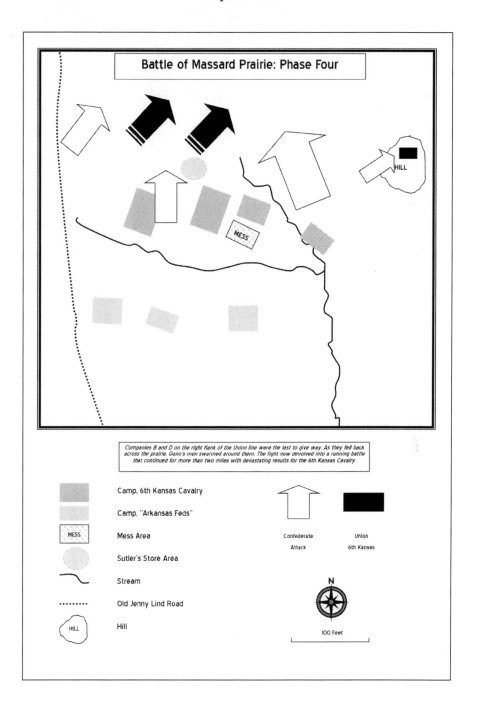

Companies B and D on the right flank of the Union line were the last to give way. As they fell back across the prairie, Gano's men swarmed around them. The fight now devolved into a running battle that continued for more than two miles with devastating results for the 6th Kansas Cavalry.

Camp, 6th Kansas Cavalry

Camp, "Arkansas Feds"

MESS — Mess Area

Sutler's Store Area

Stream

Old Jenny Lind Road

HILL — Hill

Confederate Attack

Union 6th Kansas

N

100 Feet

The Battle of Massard Prairie

The decision to retreat across the prairie moved the Federals into the open and exposed them to the full fury of Gano's mounted force. There was little else they could do, however, as they were severely outnumbered and being attacked from all directions. Staying in place would have resulted in their annihilation, while withdrawing across the prairie preserved the fight a few minutes longer. Mefford apparently was also hoping for reinforcements to come up from the nearby camp of the 14th Kansas Cavalry, but these troops could not react fast enough to save him.

The ten men sent to the left under Sergeant Goss were quickly cut off from the rest of the battalion by the charging Confederates under Folsom and Wells. Goss and his men tried to make a stand on a pronounced hilltop to the east of the camp, south of Geren Road between today's battlefield park and the Ben Geren Park golf course. They were surrounded and captured in short order and Folsom's Choctaw soldiers swarmed the top of the hill.[46]

From this vantage point, as an eyewitness attached to his command wrote, Folsom was able to obtain a good view of the whole scene of the fighting:

> *Advancing to the summit of an eminence where the Yankee balls were whizzing all around him, Col. Folsom prevailed on his Choctaws to accompany him over a broad space to the face of the enemy. The other bodies charged simultaneously, and the robbers finding themselves previously assailed in front and on both flanks, commenced a skedaddle from the rear, while others fought with desperation....*[47]

Unable to restrain themselves in the face of such a cornucopia of desperately needed supplies, some of the Confederates began to systematically loot the Federal camps, even as the fighting spread north across the open prairie. Lieutenant Burgoyne noted that, "a

---

[46] Burgoyne, July 29, 1864.
[47] Augusta, Georgia, *Chronicle & Sentinel*, October 12, 1864, p. 3, quoting an eyewitness account in the Meridian, Mississippi, *Clarion*.

number had been killed, wounded, and captured, and the enemy's stragglers were engaged in stripping them," despite the fact that an intense fight was still underway.[48]

The Federals fought and retreated across the open ground to the north until they reached a point about one-half mile from a place they called the "house on the prairie." This was a residence that once stood near the center of Massard Prairie and, because of its location, was an identifiable landmark at the time of the Civil War:

> We fought and retreated in good order until we came within half a mile of the house on the prairie, when the enemy closed in on all sides, taking many more of our men prisoners. Those that were left continued fighting and falling back to the house.[49]

As the fighting shifted north across the prairie, the Federals were able to bring the superior firepower of their rifles to bear. The Confederates, however, attempted to negate this advantage by employing an unusual tactic they had learned in combat. As the Union troops would fire a volley, the Southern troops would charge toward them on horseback, unleash a volley of their own, and then withdraw back out of range before the Federals could fire again. This process was repeated time after time as the fight moved across the open ground.[50]

According to one Confederate participant, the Union soldiers fought with unusual ferocity because they believed they were fighting for their lives:

> They fought with desperation under the impression that the Indians would murder them if they surrendered. The fight was kept up on the prairie some fifteen or twenty minutes, when the entire party was either killed or captured, with the exception of 150

[48] *Ibid.*
[49] Morehead, July 29, 1864.
[50] Burgoyne, July 29, 1864.

mounted men who effected their escape before the grove was surrendered.[51]

This claim was verified by a second Confederate participant who wrote a short time later that, "the commanding officer told us afterwards that he thought we were all Indians, and they would every one be butchered so he gave orders to his men not to surrender, but to sell their lives as dearly as possible."[52]

Lieutenant Burgoyne, on the Federal side of the fight, was among the mounted men who escaped the Confederate trap. He reported that they broke through the encircling lines during the fight on the open prairie:

> *At this time the few mounted men broke through the enemy's lines and tried to make the north side of the prairie, hotly pursued by, I should think, seventy-five or one hundred men, firing all the time. They followed to the timber, where one of their number was killed. We came in on the Greenwood road with some considerable loose stock.*[53]

Despite the escape of these men, the fight on the prairie continued to rage. A Confederate soldier saw Gano "in the thickest of the fray, directing and cheering the men, and his coolness and gallantry is the theme of the entire brigade." The unidentified eyewitness went on to note, "You can always tell his whereabouts by the cheering of the troops."[54]

The remaining Federals, unable to break through, made it as far across the open ground as the "house on the prairie" before they were pinned in place by Gano's men. Most of this area of the battlefield has been developed today and is now covered with houses, businesses and industries.

---

[51] Galveston *Weekly News*, August 17, 1864.
[52] Augusta, Georgia, *Daily Constitutionalist*, September 25, 1864, p. 1.
[53] Burgoyne, July 29, 1864.
[54] Galveston *Weekly News*, August 17, 1864.

Fearful that they would all be slaughtered, the trapped Federals initially refused to surrender and the battle quickly degenerated into an all out brawl. The Confederate eyewitness with Folsom's men wrote, "Many of our men clubbed with their guns and dealt stunning blows; several guns were in this way broken."[55]

Confederate officers finally managed to convince Mefford that he and his men would be spared if they threw down their weapons. The survivors of the command then surrendered after less than one hour of fighting:

> As it was, the men were run down and compelled to surrender, which the last of them did at the house in the middle of the prairie, Captain Mefford being with them. The men behaved splendidly, repulsing repeated charges of the enemy's cavalry, Captain Mefford doing all in his power to keep the men well in hand and stimulating them by his example.[56]

The Confederates continued to chase individual soldiers trying to escape across the prairie, but the main fighting of the battle was over. The underbrush and tall grass allowed some of the Union soldiers to escape, but others were rounded up and taken prisoner.

There is some confusion as to exactly how many Union soldiers and officers were captured in the fight. In his report of July 29, 1864, Lieutenant Burgoyne, the adjutant of the 6th Kansas, placed the total number at 120 men and two officers:

Company	Number Captured
Company B	40
Company D	18
Company E	34
Company H	21
Company L	7

---

[55] Augusta, Georgia, *Chronicle & Sentinel*, October 12, 1864.
[56] Burgoyne, July 29, 1864.

Officers	2
Total	**122**

Brigadier General John Thayer, the commander at Fort Smith, however, reported to his commanding officer in Little Rock that Major Mefford and 82 of his men had been captured. This is somewhat inexplicable, as Thayer was certainly in possession of Burgoyne's report by this time.[57]

A third figure was given in the monthly returns for Fort Smith. These reports indicated that 115 enlisted men and two officers had been lost as prisoners, a total of 117. The records of the Kansas Adjutant General's office, meanwhile, place the total number taken from the 6th Kansas Cavalry at 114 enlisted men and two officers.[58]

Confederate accounts gave slightly higher numbers. Brigadier General Cooper reported a total of 124 in his report of August 10, 1864. Southern newspaper accounts placed the number of prisoners at 127.[59]

The numbers all differ slightly and are difficult to reconcile. It is possible that the slightly higher figures given by the Confederates included some of the "Arkansas Feds" they reported as camped with the 6th Kansas Cavalry, but this cannot be confirmed through the available documentation. The Confederate numbers may also include some civilians who were in the camp at the time of the attack.

Regardless of the precise number, the 120 or so captured Federals were disarmed and pushed south across the prairie. A few of their comrades were still in hiding in the brush and luckily managed to elude capture, among them the wounded Lieutenant Morehead from Company B:

---

[57] Brig. Gen. John H. Thayer to Maj. Gen. Frederick Steele, July 30, 1864, *Official Records*, Series 1, Volume 41 (Part one), pp. 23-24.

[58] Itinerary of the District of the Frontier, *Official Records*, Series 1, Volume 41 (Part One), p. 24; Records of the Adjutant General's Office, Wichita, Kansas.

[59] Brig. Gen. Douglas H. Cooper, Report of August 10, 1864, *Official Records*, Series 1, Volume 41 (Part One), p. 31; Augusta, Georgia, *Daily Constitutionalist*, September 25, 1864; Galveston *Weekly News*, August 17, 1864.

Chapter Four

> *Before we reached the house I received a slight*
> *wound in the right thigh. Some of my men who were*
> *first captured made their escape by hiding in the thick*
> *brush, the enemy not staying to hunt for stragglers, but*
> *left immediately after the men at the house were*
> *captured, taking with them all the men who could*
> *travel.*[60]

In addition to the Federals hiding in the brush, the Confederates left the dead and seriously wounded of both sides behind, trusting in the Union troops to care for them after they reoccupied the battlefield.

From both their prisoners and the captured Federal camp, the Confederates obtained a virtual treasure trove of supplies and weaponry. General Cooper reported that Gano seized "large numbers of small arms – rifles, revolving pistols, and clothing, &c., in profusion." The eyewitness with Folsom's men placed the numbers at, "200 Sharp's rifles, 400 revolvers, hundreds of excellent saddles, a considerable number of overcoats and many other things." The estimate is reasonable considering the number of Federals in camp at the time of the attack.[61]

One of the Texas men reported that the captured supplies included 16 wagons and a large quantity of sutler's stores, but that most of these were burned since they could not be carried away. He also mentioned the capture of a few luxuries, such as cigars, in addition to the military supplies:

> *Our men had a fine opportunity to supply them-*
> *selves with pistols, overcoats, and all the luxuries of the*
> *Yankee Sutler's establishment. Your correspondent is*
> *even now solacing himself with the unwonted luxury of*
> *a good cigar.*[62]

---

[60] Morehead, July 29, 1864.
[61] Cooper, August 10, 1864; Augusta, Georgia, *Chronicle & Sentinel*, October 5, 1864.
[62] Galveston *Weekly News*, August 17, 1864.

49

The Battle of Massard Prairie

The Confederates helped themselves to what they wanted from the camp, but did not waste time. Ordered back into their saddles by General Gano, they knew that Federal reinforcements were on the way. The general still hoped to lure some of the Union troops into an ambush at Devil's Backbone, so he kept his men moving. Setting fire to the camp and sutler's store, the Confederates started back across the prairie to the safety of the mountains before Union troops could counterattack.

M. The Union Right Flank, where Gano's column attacked.

N. The 6th Kansas formed in Line of Battle across this ground.

O. Reconstructed Structure at Camp Ford, Texas (Courtesy of Randal Gilbert)

P. Site of Camp Ford (Courtesy of Randal Gilbert)

Chapter Five

Massard Prairie: Aftermath

As the Confederates withdrew from the burning camp of the 6th Kansas Cavalry and started back across the southern end of Massard Prairie, Union troops in Fort Smith were scrambling to organize a counter attack. Alerted by a courier and possibly the sound of the gunfire that a battle was underway on the prairie, Colonel W.R. Judson of the 6th Kansas pulled together such mounted forces as were available and moved in that direction. The Union reinforcements reached the northern end of the prairie just as Gano's horsemen were leaving the southern end:

> *We had scarcely began a retrograde movement before the enemy, in large force, from Fort Smith made their appearance on the prairie. They had a battery with them. Gen. Gano did not think it prudent to fight them without artillery, fatigued as the troops were, so we very, very leisurely retired before them.*[63]

The Confederates withdrew back over the same route they had used during their approach, moving slowly and making sure they could be seen by Judson's men on the other side of the prairie. They knew that McCurtain and his men were waiting at Devil's Backbone. Morale was high after the spectacular attack and the Confederates hoped the Union reinforcements would follow them.

Apparently without halting to assess the situation at the camp, Judson set out after Gano, following the Confederates up and over the mountain at Fianna Hills.

---

[63] Galveston *Weekly News*, August 17, 1864.

The Battle of Massard Prairie

*He pursued him five miles across the mountain,
ascertaining that he had nothing except the prisoners
and what could be carried on horses. The Colonel then
halted and sent five scouts forward until they came up
with the enemy's rear, which they reached about 3
o'clock p.m., near the crossing of the Poteau, about ten
miles from the camp.*[64]

Although the Union accounts make no mention of it, Southern
reports indicate that there was some skirmishing as Judson's Federals
moved up behind Gano's Confederates. The Southern soldier whose
account appeared in the Galveston *Weekly News* on August 17, 1864,
wrote that, "They followed us very cautiously a few miles, occasionally
firing on our rear, but soon drew off." No additional casualties were
reported by either side.[65]

It is unclear why Judson did not pursue the withdrawing
Confederates with more vigor, but the likely reason was that the horses
of the mounted troops at Fort Smith were in extremely poor condition.
Throughout the summer of 1864, Union officers complained to
superiors about their inability to obtain forage and the impact this was
having on their cavalry units. Judson probably also suspected that a
larger Confederate force was somewhere south of Fort Smith and may
have feared being drawn into an ambush.

Convinced that the Confederates were withdrawing, the colonel
turned back to Massard Prairie and the ransacked camp of the 6th
Kansas Cavalry. Gano's exhausted men pulled back across the
Backbone to the James Fork, a branch of the Poteau River near
Hackett, Arkansas, where they camped for the night.

Colonel Judson arrived back on the prairie to find that the
Confederates had burned about three-quarters of the extensive camp.
Material losses were heavy, but not irreplaceable. Many of the wagons
and a quantity of the quartermaster's stores at the camp were
salvaged, but more than 100 years later artifact collectors located
numerous fire-damaged items at the site.

---

[64] Fort Smith *New Era*, July 30, 1864, p. 2.
[65] Galveston *Weekly News*, August 17, 1864.

Chapter Five

In addition to the prisoners taken, the Federals reported that they lost 10 men killed and 17 wounded. Three of the wounded men died during the days following the battle, and the number of Union casualties was 13 killed and 14 wounded. The actual number captured, according to Confederate records, was 124. Of this number, 122 of wound up at the Camp Ford prison stockade in Texas. Two of the prisoners escaped during the days following the battle.

The Confederates reported their losses as 7 killed, 26 wounded and 1 missing. The Federals, however, reported finding the bodies of 12 dead Southern soldiers on the battlefield, along with 20 Confederate wounded. Five of the Southern wounded mentioned in the Confederate reports either died from mortal wounds or were killed after Gano withdrew from the prairie with his main body. Total known Confederate losses in the battle were 12 killed, 21 wounded and 1 missing.

Fifteen year old James Robert Barnes, after watching much of the battle from his uncle's front porch on the south end of the prairie, went up to the Union camp after the fighting had ended. His account indicates that the Federals mutilated the bodies of the dead Confederates:

> *Some of the Federals with the artillery were Cherokee Indians, the White soldiers called the Cherokee "Pin Indians," I do not know why they called them that, though. The Pin Indians cut a patch of scalp about the size of the palm of their hand off the top of the dead Rebels head, taking the scalp with them. After scalping the Rebels, the Federals dug a ditch wide enough to hold a man and about three feet deep and made ready to bury the Rebels.*

The origin of the name "Pins" predated the Civil War to the era shortly after the Trail of Tears when the Cherokee bitterly divided into two factions. One faction, led by future Confederate General Stand Watie, was composed largely of a branch of the nation that was intermarried with whites. The other faction was primarily composed of

Cherokee who were not. The warriors of this latter group wore crossed pins on their lapels to identify themselves, hence the name "Pins."

The alleged scalping of the Confederate dead was not mentioned in the official Union reports of the battle, but Barnes' account is convincing in its detail. He went on to describe how the Confederate dead were wrapped in blankets and buried in the trench with their hats placed over their faces.

Scalping was not that uncommon on battlefields of the Trans-Mississippi. Union officers voiced outrage following the Battle of Pea Ridge or Elkhorn Tavern in 1862 because Confederate Native American troops had allegedly scalped several dead Union soldiers. Similar allegations and reports were also made following the Red River Campaign and a number of the battles and skirmishes in present-day Oklahoma. There is little reason to doubt that these ritualistic mutilations actually took place.

Among the Confederate dead was a prominent Choctaw leader named Red Pine or William Cass. He fell while leading the charge of Folsom's men against the left flank of the Union line. General Cooper devoted space in his official report of the battle for a rare notation regarding an individual Native American soldier:

I desire in closing this part of my report to pay a passing tribute to the memory of the Rev. Tiok-homma (or Red Pine, a Choctaw, known among the whites as William Cass), who fell mortally wounded while leading the advance. This brave warrior and Christian had on every occasion displayed the highest order of courage. He served as chaplain in my old regiment, and continued in the same position through every trial, and was also distinguished as a warrior in every battle in which his regiment was engaged until he received his death wound.[66]

---

[66] Cooper, August 10, 1864.

Chapter Five

A housing development now covers a portion of the Massard Prairie battlefield, but one of the streets there is named Red Pine in honor of the brave warrior. The exact location of his grave is not known. The Union dead were buried at Fort Smith National Cemetery. Some of the bodies were later removed to their home communities, but the graves of a number of the Massard Prairie victims can still be seen at the cemetery today.

Major General S.B. Maxey, Cooper's commanding officer, notified the Trans-Mississippi Department of the successful attack just two days after the battle:

> ...A detachment about 600 strong, under the command of Brig. Gen. R.M. Gano, made up from Gano's brigade, Col. S.N. Folsom's (Second Choctaw) regiment, and Lieut. Col. J.W. Wells' battalion, attacked the Sixth Kansas Cavalry within five miles of Fort Smith, completely routing it, killing and wounding about 50, capturing 127 prisoners, about 200 Sharps rifles, and about 400 six-shooters, a number of horses, some sutler's stores, camp equipage, &c.[67]

For the poorly armed Southern troops, the captured material provided major influx of desperately needed arms and supplies. The Confederates also did not hesitate to "liberate" their prisoners of their clothing and personal possessions. The Fort Smith *New Era* reported on August 6th that a couple of the men taken prisoner at Massard Prairie had escaped and returned to camp several days earlier. "They were in a very destitute condition," the editor wrote, "the rebels, according to their mode of warfare, having stripped most of them of their clothing. One scanty meal a day was all the food they received. This is no worse, however, than the rebels fare themselves."[68]

The Southern victory on the prairie left the Federals at Fort Smith in a bad humor. On July 29th, just two days later, they took four

---

[67] Maj. Gen. S.B. Maxey to Brig. Gen. W.R. Boggs, July 30, 1864, *Official Records*, Series 1, Volume 41, Part One, p. 29.
[68] Fort Smith *New Era*, August 6, 1864, p. 2.

The Battle of Massard Prairie

Confederate guerillas that had been captured following a raid near Fayetteville to a hilltop outside the defensive works and executed them. Union authorities had accused, tried and convicted them of murder:

> *In April last, in company with twenty of more accomplices, they murdered eight Federal soldiers of the 1ˢᵗ Ark. Cav., who were herding horses near Fayetteville, Ark. They approached our men dressed in the uniform of U.S. Soldiers, and pretending to belong to the 14ᵗʰ Kansas Cav., completely throwing them off their guard. That point gained, they suddenly and without a moment's warning fired upon them, and killing eight out of ten.*
>
> *A Union citizen, named John Brown, was also killed by the miscreants at his own house at about the same time.*[69]

The men were identified by the editor of the Fort Smith *New Era* as A.J. Copeland, James H. Rowden, John Norwood and William Carey. At least three of the men – Copeland, Norwood and Carey – were members of regular Confederate units from Arkansas. Accompanied by spiritual advisers, they were seated on their own coffins in the backs of wagons. Preceded by the Provost Marshal, Captain J.O. Judson of the 6ᵗʰ Kansas Cavalry, along with regimental musicians and a firing squad of 64 men from the 13ᵗʰ Kansas Infantry, and followed by additional guards, the men were carried to a hilltop off modern Towson Avenue near today's Sparks Hospital. There they were placed in a line, each man next to his coffin, and the members of the firing squad formed three sides of a hollow square around them while other soldiers and citizens looked on from a distance:

> *The Judge Advocate of the District, Lieut. Whicher, then read to them the charges and findings of the*

---

[69] *Ibid.*, p. 3.

*military commission, after which the condemned
kneeled down with the chaplains, and Rev. Mr. Stringer
offered a short and appropriate prayer. At the
conclusion of it the officers and others about the
condemned shook hands with them and, bidding them a
final farewell, retired, except the Judge Advocate, who
remained till their eyes were bandaged and hands tied.
By this time all of the unfortunate men showed signs of
mental distress. Carey and Copeland prayed audibly
and with great force. Norwood started a hymn, and was
still singing, in a low voice, when the death volley sent
his soul to eternity. Carey, on shaking hands with the
Judge Advocate, remarked, "Judge, I hope to meet you
in Heaven." At length all the preparations were
completed, and in another moment or two forty-eight
muskets were pointed at the culprits.*[70]

While sixteen members of the firing squad held their fire in case
the first round failed in its object, the other 48 men unleashed a volley
on the four prisoners. Half of the guns were loaded and half fired
blanks so that none of the members of the squad could be sure whether
they had fired a shot that resulted in the death of another man by
execution. In closing his account of the incident, the *New Era* editor
blamed the Confederates for the tragic scene:

*The most painful reflection awakened by the sad
ceremony was that selfish, faithless and traitorous
citizens should have stirred up a strife that precipitates
into the vortex of crime, ignominy and ruin so many of
the young men of our once peaceful, prosperous and
happy country.*[71]

If the Confederates were aware of the executions, they did not
mention them in their immediate reports. Several soldiers did write

[70] *Ibid.*
[71] *Ibid.*

letters to family members shortly after the Battle of Massard Prairie. Among these was J.H. Toliver of the 30th Texas Cavalry (1st Texas Partisan Rangers), who wrote to his wife mourning the loss of his friend, Private W.W. Jayroe:

> *I have got Mr. Jayroe's horse, saddle and bridle, blankets, saddle riders and clothes. I think it is the intention for them to be sent home. I will use my influence that way if they are give up to me to take care of. I will do the best that I can with them. Mr. Jayroe had received a slight wound in the thigh before he was killed tho he fought on as brave as a lion until he was killed. I feel it my duty to inform Mrs. Jayroe of Mr. Jayroe's death as soon as possible. You will let her know of his death as soon as you can. I couldn't miss a brother worse than I do Mr. Jayroe.*[72]

Jayroe's horse and personal effects apparently were sent home to his wife in Texas. A note attached to the preserved copy of Toliver's letter mentions that Jayroe's wife "knew that her husband was dead when she saw his horse tied to the fence."[73]

Despite such heart-felt losses, however, the raid was enormously successful for the Confederates. Pleased with the outcome of his strategy and General Gano's decisions on the field, General Cooper immediately ordered his troops to prepare for additional such actions. One day after the battle, he instructed Brigadier General Stand Watie to attack an isolated party of Federals north of the Arkansas River:

> *On the 28th Brigadier-General Watie was directed to send 200 picked men, under dashing officers, across the Arkansas River for the purpose of breaking up and burning a camp of Federals engaged in cutting hay and pasturing stock on Blackburn's Prairie. It was determined, also, to make demonstration on Fort*

---

[72] J.H. Toliver to C.H. Toliver, July 28, 1864.
[73] *Ibid.*, Attached note at end of letter.

*Smith, thereby creating a diversion in favor of Watie's
scouts; ascertain at the same time, if possible, the
strength of the enemy, and to cover the removal of
Southern families from Sebastian County along the
line.*[74]

The planned attack failed, however, because the Arkansas River
was too high for the Confederates to get across. Instead, Cooper
combined Watie's men with the rest of his command and prepared to
move up for a demonstration against Fort Smith:

*On the 29th Lieutenant-Colonel McCurtain was
directed to hold his battalion in readiness at Double
Springs to march with General Gano and cooperate
with his brigade on the day following. Brigadier-
General Watie, with the effective men of his brigade
present, was ordered to move up to Scullyville Prairie,
and the Choctaw Brigade, under Col. S.N. Folsom,
Wells' battalion , and a section of Howell's battery to
the same place. General Watie having reported the
river too full to cross, the detachments under Colonel
Bell and Colonel Adair were ordered to join General
Watie at Scullyville. Major Burnet, with his battalion of
sharpshooters, the most of the artillery, and the train
were ordered back toward Riddle's. The whole, except
Major Burnet's command, encamped on Scullyville
Prairie night of the 30th, while General Gano and
McCurtain bivouacked at James' Fork, near Wall's
Mill.*[75]

As Cooper assembled his forces for a second attack, the Federals
were preoccupied with the executions of the four Confederate guerillas.
Despite the disaster at Massard Prairie, there is no indication that

---

[74] Brig. Gen. Douglas H. Cooper, Report of August 10, 1864, *Official Records*, Series 1,
Volume 41, Part One, p. 32.
[75] *Ibid., pp. 32-33.*

they increased the number or strength of their picket posts south of town. The oversight would once again allow the Confederates to approach without detection until the last minute.

Gen. Douglas H. Cooper, C.S.A.

Gen. Richard M. Gano, C.S.A.

Gen. John M. Thayer, U.S.A.

Col. W.R. Judson, U.S.A.

Chapter Six

The Battle of Fort Smith

General Cooper's plan for the demonstration in front of Fort Smith called for a quadruple approach to the Union lines. General Watie would move sections of his men up the main or Fort Towson road (today's Towson Avenue) and the Line or Garrison road at the same time and approach the Federal entrenchments from the South. Cooper would follow shortly behind with the main body, prepared to snap up any Union force that came out to battle Watie's men. General Gano, meanwhile, was ordered to move to the right with a large force and push once again into Massard Prairie, attacking any Federals he might find there. A fourth and smaller column, commanded by Major James Burnet, was ordered to move up the River road from Scullyville and penetrate the Poteau Bottom opposite Fort Smith to divert the attention of the Federals and fire into the main garrison.[76]

Cooper had no intention of launching a full attack against the main fort or of assaulting the Federal earthworks. His plan, instead, was to demonstrate in force outside the works, capture any Union troops who might be found in the open and, hopefully, draw some of the Federals out of their fortifications where they could be successfully attacked. By advancing on four fronts, he hoped to disorient Fort Smith's defenders and trick them into unnecessarily exposing themselves.

The advance began at sunrise on the morning of July 31, 1864. Major Burnet with the 2nd Creek Regiment, accompanied by a few Cherokee under Captain Samuel H. Gunter, pushed up the River road into Poteau Bottom. This force was accompanied by Captain B.W. Marston, Cooper's assistant adjutant-general. Although the Poteau River was too high to allow them to do much damage, they moved

---

[76] Brig. Gen. Douglas H. Cooper, Report of August 10, 1864, *Official Records*, Series 1, Volume 41, Part One, p. 33.

through the woods and reached the riverbank opposite the main garrison without opposition. From this point the Native American troops opened fire on the fort and, according to Cooper, created "great excitement and some consternation."[77]

General Gano, meanwhile, moved off to the east and occupied a hilltop overlooking Massard Prairie. Most likely this was the same position from which he had surveyed the prairie prior to the battle on the 27th, undoubtedly somewhere along the ridge of today's Fianna Hills subdivision. From this vista he sent Lieutenant Colonel Jack McCurtain and his Choctaw battalion down onto the prairie to attract the attention of the Federals and draw them out into the open. Camp Judson, partially destroyed during the Battle of Massard Prairie, had evidently been abandoned over the preceding three days. McCurtain was unable to draw out any significant enemy force, but did succeed in capturing "3 regular Federal soldiers and 8 Arkansans." He also captured several horses and a drove of beef cattle.[78]

As the operations to the east and west were underway, Cooper moved with the main body up the Fort Towson Road from a jumping off point at "Wat. Folsom's place" near Cedar Prairie. This was on the southern edge of the modern Fort Smith metropolitan area, but at the time of the Civil War was a rural area more than five miles south of the limits of the town. Much of the area where the battle would be fought is now industrial in nature and only faint traces of the original landscape can still be seen.

The Fort Towson Road entered Fort Smith via the route of today's Towson Avenue. One of the earthen redoubts constructed to defend the town had been built along this road on an elevated spot then known as "Negro Hill." The hill can still be seen off Dodson Avenue between Towson and Wheeler in Fort Smith. Labeled Battery Number Two in Union reports, the position was flanked by lines of rifle pits that stretched to the banks of the Poteau River on the west and curved along the ridgeline to the east to connect with another battery near Immaculate Conception Catholic Church. Most of the entrenchments

---

[77] *Ibid.*, p. 35.
[78] *Ibid.*, pp. 34-35.

Chapter Six

have long since vanished, but a small section of rifle pits can still be
seen off Dodson Avenue west of Towson.

To provide advance warning of an attack via this route, the
Federals had posted a detachment from the 6th Kansas Cavalry near
Gum Springs about four and one half miles south of Fort Smith. Second
Lieutenant Levi F. Stewart was commanding this encampment on the
morning of July 31st:

> Being stationed on outpost duty on the Texas road
> about four miles and a half from Fort Smith, Ark.,
> about 11 [a.m.] of the morning of July 31, 1864, hearing
> my pickets firing, I immediately mounted my men,
> numbering thirty-five in all, and started to learn the
> cause of the firing. After proceeding about half a mile I
> met my pickets coming toward me on a run and a
> number of the enemy following them, at which I halted
> and formed a line, and after exchanging shots with the
> enemy I found they were too strong for the number of
> men under my command and I [was] forced to fall back
> toward Fort Smith, Ark., exchanging shots continually
> with the enemy. I was forced to fall back some two
> miles and a half. I halted and formed into line and
> found the enemy had halted. During the skirmishing
> one of my men was either killed or taken prisoner and
> one wounded.[79]

Watie's men quickly overwhelmed Lieutenant Stewart's small
command. Advancing simultaneously on the Fort Towson and Line or
Garrison roads, Watie's troops struck hard and fast:

> General Watie executed the order given him with
> his accustomed gallantry and promptness, sending
> Colonel Bell, with the First Cherokee Regiment, on the
> main road and Colonel Adair on the road to the left

[79] 2nd Lt. Levi F. Stewart, Report of August 2, 1864, *Official Records*, Series 1, Volume 41,
Part One, pp. 25-26.

known as the Line road, both detachments charging with the gallant impetuosity for which they and their men are noted. He not only routed the Federal pickets, but ran them up to the line of their intrenchments near Fort Smith, and returning the men sat down to the plentiful dinner just prepared for the Federals at their camp.[80]

In addition to a "plentiful dinner," the Confederates seized the camp and garrison equipage at the Federal outpost. Although Union officers did not estimate the value of this seizure, Confederate reports indicate that it was quite large. Cooper later estimated the value of materials captured at $130,000 (in Confederate currency).[81]

To support the attack, the Confederates ordered forward artillery to an elevated position overlooking a field that separated Watie's men from a hill about one mile in front the Federal entrenchments. The light guns consisted of a section from Captain Howell's battery and a section from Lee's light howitzer battery. The former was commanded by Captain Howell himself, while the latter was under Captain John T. Humphreys. Wells' Texas battalion, the Choctaw Brigade and the 1st Creek Regiment moved up in support of the guns.

Despite their initial surprise, the Federal troops rallied quickly after reaching their main line and soon advanced to the hill separating their entrenchments from the main body of Confederates:

A brisk fire of skirmishers was kept up for some time, the rebels at the same time throwing shells from a couple of howitzers. A part of the 2d Kan. Battery, Capt. Smith, promptly took position about a mile in advance of Fort No. 2, supported by two companies of the 1st Kansas colored, and just in time to prevent the rebels from occupying the same hill. The enemy had

---

[80] Brig. Gen. Douglas H. Cooper, Report of August 10, 1864, *Official Records,* Series 1, Volume 41, Part One, p. 33.
[81] *Ibid.*, p. 34.

fired a number of shots before our guns were in position.[82]

The Confederates described the attack in similar terms. According to Cooper's report, Captain Humphreys was advanced forward with his light battery to open fire on the Federals, who were positioned about 600-800 yards ahead:

> *The enemy were driven back and took up a position upon a high ridge under cover of the guns at Negro Hill. Captain Humphreys, with his light battery, followed them and kept up a galling fire, which I could plainly see told with considerable effect among the cavalry on the road.*[83]

The Confederate fire was not particularly effective, but Cooper had no way of knowing for sure. Colonel Judson of the 6th Kansas Cavalry was wounded in the left leg by a shell fragment, but remained on the field throughout the battle.

Once the Federals were able to move their own field artillery forward, the balance of power on the field shifted and the superiority of the Union guns soon forced Humphreys to withdraw his pieces:

> *The enemy soon brought up a four gun battery (Rabb's, I suppose) and commenced a furious cannonade upon our light howitzers, the shot and shell passing harmlessly over our heads for some time. Captain Humphreys, being so unequally matched, was ordered to withdraw, and in the act of doing so a shell exploded directly amid the battery horses, killing 3, wounding 1, cutting off the leg of one of the men. Another shot swept off the head from the shoulders of one of Gano's men. My escort, under Lieutenant*

---

[82] Fort Smith *New Era*, August 6, 1864, p. 2.
[83] Brig. Gen. Douglas H. Cooper, Report of August 10, 1864, *Official Records*, Series 1, Volume 41, Part One, p. 34.

Johnson, succeeded, under a very heavy fire, in cutting the dead horses loose from the gun and leading it off with one horse, assisted by the men pushing the carriage along, without further loss.[84]

The editor of the Fort Smith *New Era*, writing a few days later, described seeing the Confederate artillery horses, "dead and crippled with their harness on, on the field of action." Also found on the field was a canteen, "cut all to pieces by shot and covered with blood." The writer assumed, correctly, that "the owner of it must also have been terribly mangled."[85]

The arrival of the superior Union artillery quickly brought the Confederate demonstration to a close:

It was now nearly dark. The enemy's infantry quite near. The undergrowth being thick, their numbers and strength could not be ascertained. Numerous roads by which we could be flanked and the infantry operate to advantage upon my cavalry gave them great advantage. Orders were therefore given to withdraw....[86]

Gano's brigade formed the rear guard of the Confederate force and burned the captured Union outpost. A portion of the Cherokee troops off the left flank could not be located with the orders to withdraw due to the heavy undergrowth on the battlefield, but they quickly deduced the situation and pulled back as well. His force reassembled, Cooper withdrew to Cedar Prairie and camped for the night.[87]

As the Confederates pulled back, sharpshooters from the Native American units continued to hover around the edges of Fort Smith. Some fired from Poteau Bottom across the river into the main garrison and others kept up a sporadic skirmish with the Federal troops in front of Fort Number 2.

---

[84] *Ibid.*
[85] Fort Smith *New Era*, August 6, 1864, p.2.
[86] Cooper, Report of August 10, 1864, p. 34.
[87] *Ibid.*

Chapter Six

The sniping, combined with nightfall, kept the Federals on edge and prevented them from probing forward to find out what was happening with the Confederate main body. The only Union troops who tried to reach the Southern lines that night were deserters. Several entered the Southern camps, providing information on the wounding of Colonel Judson and the status of the enemy defenses.

Total casualties for the day were remarkably light. One of Gano's men had been killed. Five other Confederate soldiers were wounded, among them a Cherokee artilleryman named Wammack who soon died from his wounds. Estimates of Federal losses vary. The Fort Smith *New Era* reported one killed, one wounded and one captured, apparently not including Colonel Judson. The monthly returns of the District of the Frontier, however, list "Colonel Judson wounded, ten enlisted men killed and wounded."[88]

The demonstration proved highly effective. Cooper was able to achieve his original goal of giving pro-Southern families in the area a chance to leave Fort Smith under the protection of his troops. In addition, however, his men inflicted severe terror on pro-Union families living in the area:

> *Many of the Fort Smith rebels were among the assailants, and would, no doubt, have been highly gratified if they could have come in.*
>
> *The Union families in the vicinity of the place suffered severely. Many of their houses were burned down, and all plundered more or less.*[89]

Cooper alluded to the devastation wrought on local Unionist families in his report. Just as his men had struck hard at the people they considered traitors during the advance on Massard Prairie, they did so again when they pushed up to the defenses of Fort Smith:

---

[88] Fort Smith *New Era*, August 6, 1864, p. 2; *Official Records*, Series I, Volume 41, Part One, pp. 24, 34.
[89] Fort Smith *New Era*, August 6, 1864, p. 2.

The Battle of Massard Prairie

> *The demonstration in front of Fort Smith resulted in driving the whole Union population of Sebastian County within the town, thus increasing the enemy's embarrassments on account of food, and in satisfying me that the enemy was weaker and more demoralized than I had anticipated.*[90]

The Confederates remained at Cedar Prairie until the next morning and then, having achieved their immediate goals, began their withdrawal away from Fort Smith. Watie's command crossed the Poteau and continued on to Scullyville, while the rest of the men returned south to their camps at Buck Creek.

As they moved back into the Choctaw Nation, Cooper and his men were surprised to hear the sound of artillery fire at Fort Smith. They soon learned that it was caused by "Captain Gunter and a few Cherokees amusing themselves by shooting across Poteau." In an attempt to disperse them, the Federals rolled cannon out of the main garrison and opened fire across the river. Gunter and his men simply changed positions and continued their harassment, moving around in the woods and annoying the Union soldiers for much of the day. Cooper reported that he could hear the cannon fire from as far as 25 miles away.[91]

---

[90] Cooper, Report of August 10, 1864, p. 36.
[91] *Ibid.*

Gen. Stand Watie, C.S.A.

The only Native American to achieve the rank of brigadier general in the service of the Confederacy, Stand Watie was not on the field at Massard Prairie but fought during the Battle of Fort Smith a few days later. Of the many generals who served the South, he was the last to lay down his arms.

W.H. Webb, 31st Texas Cavalry

Courtesy of David Howard

J.H. Asher, 6th Kansas Cavalry

Wounded at Massard Prairie

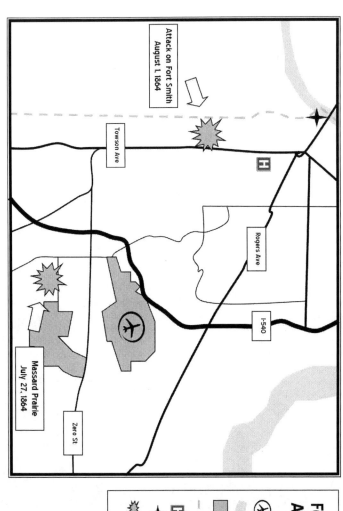

Attack on Fort Smith
August 1, 1864

Towson Ave

Rogers Ave

I-540

Massard Prairie
July 27, 1864

Zero St

N

2 Miles

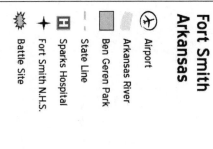

Fort Smith
Arkansas

✈ Airport

Arkansas River

Ben Geren Park

State Line

H Sparks Hospital

✦ Fort Smith N.H.S.

Battle Site

Chapter Seven

Concluding the Action

The Confederate attack at Massard Prairie and demonstration on Fort Smith were major successes for Cooper's command. Not only had the Southern troops succeeded in killing, wounding or capturing numerous enemy soldiers, they had also captured desperately needed horses, cattle, commissary supplies and arms. Two significant Union outposts had been overrun and destroyed, resulting in hundreds of thousands of dollars in losses to the Federal forces at Fort Smith. More importantly, Cooper, Gano and Watie had virtually hemmed the Union force within the fortifications, clearing the way for the highly successful Cabin Creek expedition that followed a short time later.

Some idea of the degree to which the Federals felt themselves on the defensive following the bold attacks can be found from reading General Thayer's monthly report:

> *I still think their object is to hold this force here, and also to make raids across the river between here and Gibson when the river is fordable, as it soon will be. I have no fears as to this place or Gibson. I may have to withdraw the troops from Clarksville for the reason that I shall have to keep the trains running from Fort Gibson to Fort Scott, and shall have to strengthen the escorts on that route, and also guard the fords between here and Gibson. I also have to furnish a large force to guard the parties putting up hay. My cavalry are almost useless as cavalry for want of serviceable horses...The force in my front is from 5,000 to 7,000, nearly all mounted. I am only prevented from moving out and fighting them by the want of cavalry and*

73

artillery horses. I could not move my batteries twenty
miles this hot weather before half of the horses would
give out.[92]

Thayer would soon have reason to learn just how prophetic his summary of the situation had been. Having penned Thayer's forces within their defenses, Cooper sent Gano and Watie north across the Arkansas River just two weeks after the attacks on Fort Smith. They overwhelmed and slaughtered a detachment of Federals guarding a hay-cutting party near today's Wagoner, Oklahoma, and then, on September 19, 1864, stunned a major Union train of 300 supply wagons and 1,800 mules and horses at Cabin Creek in the Cherokee Nation. Scattering and destroying what they couldn't carry away, the Confederates returned to headquarters with 130 wagon loads of supplies and 740 mules. It was one of the great supply train captures of the war and resulted in the issuance of special commendations to Gano, Watie and their men by the Confederate Congress in Richmond.

The Confederate attacks on Fort Smith opened the door for the dramatic victory at Cabin Creek. The two expeditions combined to inflict more than $2,000,000 in damage to the Union war effort on the western frontier. Other than Florida, the Arkansas-Oklahoma borderlands comprised the one area where Southern forces demonstrated major success during the final months of the Civil War. General Stand Watie was the last Confederate general to lay down his arms and was said to have been shocked by the news that Confederate forces in the east had been defeated.

In addition to clearing the way for the Cabin Creek expedition, the fighting at Massard Prairie and Fort Smith resulted in the mass evacuation of dozens of pro-Union families from the area. The movement was so sudden and so large that the Confederates thought at first that the entire garrison might be withdrawing:

...I determined to send General Watie back to Poteau
Bottom and General Gano to Massard Prairie for the

---

[92] *Official Records*, Series I, Volume 41, Part One, p. 24.

*purpose of ascertaining whether the enemy were really
evacuating, and to hurry them out in case such proved
to be the case. Parties who had seen the movements on
Arkansas River were so confident that an evacuation
would take place that (contrary to my own impression)
I concluded to order up my trains and remain. It was
soon ascertained that the exodus of the Union families
and baggage was the solution of appearances on
Arkansas River, and we moved back slowly, resting
wherever grass and water could be found....*[93]

The *New Era* confirmed the evacuation, reporting that a long train
of civilian refugees had headed north for Kansas, escorted by Union
soldiers. The flight was a sad commentary on the horrible nature of the
times.

The days of the Confederacy, however, were numbered and the
successes on the western frontier would do nothing to alter the
inevitable. The rough and tumble character of the Civil War in the
region lingered on long after the end of the war.

The Indian Nations of modern Oklahoma were overrun by raiders
and outlaws following the close of the war. Without the presence of
large bodies of both Union and Confederate troops to subdue them,
these criminals rampaged through the region terrifying citizens.
Murder and robbery were the watchwords of the day. It was not until
U.S. District Judge Isaac C. Parker assumed the bench for the Western
District of Arkansas that the tide began to change. From an office and
courtroom in the old fort buildings at Fort Smith, Parker and his
deputies brought law and order to the frontier, executing dozens of
hardened criminals on the gallows of Fort Smith. Parker's deputy
marshals were unique in the history of 19th century America because
they represented all of the races present in the region and included
men from many different backgrounds. They provided the inspiration
for such fictional books and movies as *True Grit* and *Hang Em' High*
and many lost their lives in the line of duty.

---

[93] Cooper, Report of August 10, 1864.

The Battle of Massard Prairie

The original military post of Fort Smith is today the Fort Smith National Historic Site. An outstanding place to learn more about life on the early frontier, the park preserves two surviving structures of the Civil War fort, as well as a reconstruction of Parker's gallows, the late 19th century Federal jail facility and the site of Belle Point at the confluence of the Poteau and Arkansas Rivers. National Park Service personnel are available to provide information on all aspects of the significant history of the old fort.

The site of most of the fighting of the July 31, 1864, demonstration on Fort Smith is now heavily industrialized. A small section of rifle pits near the site of Fort Number 2 has been preserved, but most of the battlefield is developed. It is still possible, however, to view the terrain from the hilltop at the intersection of Towson and Dodson in Fort Smith and see most of the area where the fight took place. There are no markers or other interpretive facilities.

A key area of the Massard Prairie battlefield, however, has been saved. Thanks to a community effort that involved partners as divergent as local artifact collectors, historians, businessmen and government leaders, most of the site of Camp Judson is now the Massard Prairie Battlefield Park. Located near the intersection of Red Pine and Morgan Way off Geren Road, the park is a work in progress. Development at the time of this writing includes a short walking trail, small signs pointing out the locations of the mess, parade ground and individual company camps, a memorial flagstaff and the monument placed by the United Daughters of the Confederacy.

Walking the trail through the park, it is possible to view much of the scene of the initial action of the Battle of Massard Prairie. The small branch that flowed along the south side of the camp can still be seen, although it is dry most of the year. The Union line of battle was formed along the slight ridge preserved within the park and the Confederate attacks came up from the southeast, south and southwest. Although the open prairie immediately north of the park is under private ownership and posted, it is possible to look across the ground from the northern edge of the park and see what remains of the terrain across which the 6th Kansas Cavalry attempted to retreat. Enough of the original prairie remains to provide visitors with a good understanding of the original appearance of the land.

The rest of Massard Prairie is largely developed today. A portion of the ground is occupied by the Fort Smith Regional Airport, which boasts what may be the nicest terminal of any airport in the United States. Some of the rest is contained in Ben Geren Park, a large and popular recreational complex operated by Sebastian County. Although much the prairie is now covered with businesses, industries and residential areas, some areas of open ground remain and cows even graze in one spot along Interstate 540. From the surrounding hills, the vast "bowl" of the prairie can still be seen and it is easy to picture it as it once was, a huge open area, dotted with trees and brush.

Fort Smith is far removed from its appearance at the time of the Civil War. Now the second largest city in Arkansas, the community is developing a growing appreciation for its heritage and historic sites. Home to a growing heritage tourism industry, the city boasts museums, wonderful park areas and historic homes and buildings. Fort Smith was recently selected as the new home of the national museum for the U.S. Marshals Service, a dream that will become a reality over the next few years. In addition, the city is an important gateway to the Ozark and Ouachita Mountains. The historic lands of eastern Oklahoma that once comprised the Indian Territory are just across the river. The proximity of so many historic and natural resources place Fort Smith in the center of a wonderful region for exploring spectacular scenery and unparalleled history.

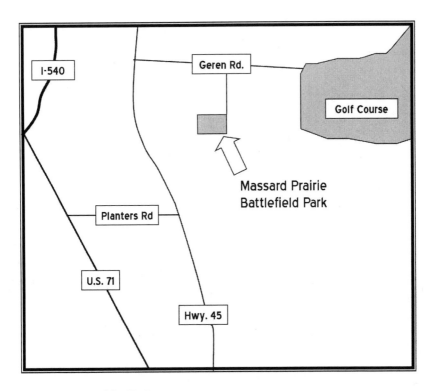

Massard Prairie, Today

A section of the site of the battle has been preserved at Massard Prairie Battlefield Park in Fort Smith. The park is located just off Geren Road in the southeast quadrant of the city.

A few areas of prairie can still be seen in the area surrounding the park, but much of the battlefield is now covered by modern industrial, commercial and residential development.

1 Mile

Chapter Eight

Massard Prairie in the News

Although it was a relatively small engagement fought on the far western frontier, the Battle of Massard Prairie received a surprising amount of coverage in newspapers of the time, both North and South. These accounts include eyewitness reports and additional detail on casualties that greatly expand our knowledge of the events at Fort Smith in July of 1864.

The following transcriptions are provided as a sample of some of the coverage provided by the nation's editors during the weeks and months after the battle and includes most of the original articles repeated by other newspapers across the country:

Fort Smith *New Era*
July 30, 1864

REBEL ATTACK ON OUR OUTPOSTS

Last Wednesday, July 27th, about sunrise a strong force of rebels under General Gano, consisting of the 30th, and part of the 31st regiments Texas Cavalry, Col. Well's battalion, and Folsom's and Walker's regiments of Choctaws of Cooper's brigade, in all, about two thousand men, made an attack on a battalion of the 6th Kansas cavalry, numbering about 200 men and commanded by Maj. Mefford of that regiment on Mazard prairie, about seven miles from town.

Our men fought most heroically against overwhelming odds, retreating slowly towards town and contending every inch of ground. They were however, at last completely surrounded and overpowered and a number taken prisoners, among whom were Maj. Mefford and

Lieut. De Friese. Ten of our men were killed, 15 wounded; the rest fought their way through.

The rebels lost 12 killed and 20 wounded.

As soon as the news of the attack reached Headquarters, Col. Judson, 6th Kans. Cav., hastened to the scene of action with a mounted force, but found that the enemy had left an hour and a half before his arrival. He pursued him five miles across the mountain, ascertaining that he had nothing except the prisoners and what could be carried on horses. The Colonel then halted and sent five scouts forward until they came up with the enemy's rear, which they reached about 3 o'clock, p.m., near the crossing of the Poteau, about ten miles from the camp. The colonel then returned to the camp and found that the enemy had burned about three fourths of the camp and had left in a great hurry, leaving large quantities of Quartermaster's stores and transportation unharmed.

Fort Smith *New Era*
July 30, 1864

A dead mule belonging to a Memphis citizen, was being hauled out of the lines the other day when a bayonet thrust revealed the fact that the carcass contained 60,000 percussion caps, a quantity of ammunition, and other contraband articles, which some rebel sympathizer had taken this means of smuggling.

Fort Smith *New Era*
August 6, 1864

Returned from Captivity: Several of the men taken prisoners in the fight on the 27th ult., on Mazzard Prairie, have made their escape from their captors and came in a few days ago. They belong to the 6th Kansas Cavalry. They were in a very destitute condition, the rebels, according to their mode of warfare, having stripped them of most of their clothing. One scanty meal a day was all the food they received. This is no worse, however, than the rebels fare themselves.

They confirm the previous estimates made of the rebels, setting them down at ten thousand, with ten pieces of artillery.

Houston (Texas) Telegraph
August 3, 1864

BY TELEGRAPH.

Special to the Telegraph

Shreveport, August 1st, 1864.

HEADQUARTERS FORCES DIST.
INDIAN TERRITORY, JULY 28, 1864

Captain: Gen. Gano, Col. Folsom and Lieut. Col. Wells, with detachments of their respective commands, about six hundred men in all, fell upon and demolished the Sixth Kansas cavalry yesterday morning in their camp within five miles of Fort Smith.

We have about one hundred stand of Sharp's rifles, four hundred six shooters, besides every horse being loaded down with plunder, camp equipage, sutler's stores, &c., one hundred and twenty-seven prisoners, including the major commanding and other officers, the fruits of the expedition.

Gen. Cooper had directed before to attack and destroy or capture the Arkansas home guards stationed in this vicinity, but the Kansas Sixth having moved out afterwards, they were not attacked., but stampeded in the melee. Our loss, 8 killed and wounded. Enemy's loss heavy, fully seven times as great, having had four fifths of the command mounted to pursue in an open prairie for three miles. Gen. Cooper is establishing a line in front, or he would have written this dispatch himself.

Very respectfully,
[Signed] B.W. Marston, Capt. & A.A.G.
To Capt. S.M. Scott, A.A.G., Indian Territory.

Daily *Constitutional Union* (Washington, D.C.)
August 6, 1864

LATE FROM THE SOUTHWEST.

FIVE HUNDRED REBELS DEFEATED NEAR FORT SMITH, ARK.

FEDERAL FORCES PURSUING THEM.

REBELS BEING CONVERTED IN GEN. FISK'S DEPARTMENT.

St. Louis, August 6. – A dispatch dated Fort Smith, Arkansas, first instant, says the rebels under Cooper, Gande, and Standwait, five hundred strong, with twelve pieces of artillery, moved up yesterday with an intention of attacking Fort Smith.

General Thayer went out, met the enemy a short distance from the fortifications, and completely routed them.

Our cavalry is still pursuing.

Our loss is very small. That of the rebels is unknown.

Dallas (Texas) *Herald*
August 6, 1864

Victory near Fort Smith. – We are indebted J.K.P. Campbell, C.S. of this District for the following dispatch, received by Wednesday....

HEAD Q'RS DIST. INDIAN TERRITORY.

FT. TOWNSON, July 30, 1864.

On the 27th inst. a detachment under Gen. Gano, ------- and Lt. Col. Wells, about 600 strong, attacked and demolished the 6th Kansas Cavalry, within – miles from Fort Smith. The results of the victory are --- prisoners, including the Major Commanding, --- officers, 200 Sharp's Rifles, 400 revolvers, --- horses loaded down with plunder, camp -----, equipage &c. A portion of the com------- mounted and pushed the enemy three miles. Our loss was 8 killed and a proportionate number wounded. The loss of the enemy was even ---- greater. The expedition was organized to attack a camp of Ark. Militia, but in the mean time the 6th Kansas Regiment had moved out & were ----- the Militia stampeded and escaped.

A.C. Eliason.
Gen. Maxey's Staff.

The *Ohio Daily Statesman*
August 8, 1864

The Rebels Routed at Fort Smith
  -   From Missouri.

St. Louis, Aug. 6 – A dispatch dated Fort Smith, Ark., August 1st, says the rebels under Cooper, Gano and Standart, five hundred strong, with twelve pieces of artillery, moved up yesterday with the intention of attacking Fort Smith. Gen. Thayer moved out to meet the enemy a short distance from the fort, and completely routed them. Our cavalry is still pursuing. Our loss was very small; that of the enemy is unknown.

Houston *Telegraph*
August 24, 1864

The following is a list of the killed and wounded of Gurley's Regiment, 30th Texas Cavalry, commanded by Captain Oscar J. Downs, in the battle of Diamond Grove, near Fort Smith, Ark., on the 27th ult.

Co. A – Killed: Serg't Plk Levy. Wounded: private Asa Johnson, severely, in leg.

Co. B – Wounded: Capt. J.P. Morris, slightly, in side; Serg't G.W. Jackson, severely, in shoulder.

Co. C – Wounded: private Wm Hensley, slightly, in elbow.

Co. E – Killed: private John Small. Wounded: W.E. Richardson, severely, in hand.

Co. F – Killed: Capt. C.C. McCurry, private Wm. Jayrow. Wounded: privates W.R. Baker, severely, in thigh, A.J. Wiley, slightly, in breast.

Co. H – Wounded: Captain Jackson Puckett, slightly, in foot, Lieut. J.C. Snead, severely, in shoulder.

Total killed, 4; wounded: 9.

W.H. Everitt, Lieut. and
Acting Adjutant, 30th T.C.

Houston (Texas) *Telegraph*
September 9, 1864

Gano's Brigade, C.N.,
Aug. 6th, 1864.

Ed. Telegraph.- Gurley's regiment has undergone as many privations; has endured as many hardships, has done some as hard fighting, and has had less notice before the public, and a smaller share of glory given to it than any regiment west of the Mississippi. The reasons for this are numerous, first, it has no newspaper correspondent; second it is serving in a district which claims but little public attention, and third, its fights have always, from the very nature of the service, been on a small scale compared with other parts of the service.

Chapter Eight

At Rossville, Arkansas, last spring, Gurley's regiment fought and whipped the 6th Kansas regiment, which is regarded as the best regiment the Yankees have on this side of the Mississippi. At Poison Springs again only a few weeks later, it fought the same regiment with the same result, and at Diamond Grove, near Fort Smith on 26th July it fought the same regiment with a far more glorious result than ever. In this, however, other regiments were engaged, but in honor to Gurley's regiment, and to Capt. Down's who commanded it with such unsurpassed noble daring and heroism, it should be known that out of the 127 prisoners taken on the occasion, 100 of them were captured by this regiment; that this regiment alone, fought the retreating regiment on the open (Mazzard) prairie one and a half miles; and they captured more arms and accoutrements, and lost five times as many in killed and wounded, as all the balance of the brigade added together.

BOB.

Houston (Texas) *Telegraph*
August 16, 1864

We traveled nearly all night, halting about two hours, just before day, to arrange plans, and give the men a little rest, soon after sunrise we drove in the enemy's pickets, passed over a high mountain, and came down into Mazzard prairie, four miles from Fort Smith. At the far end of this prairie, some one and a half miles from the foot of the mountain, we discovered a beautiful island of timber, known as the Diamond or Picnic Grove, at the north end of which we spotted our game, making hasty preparations to give us a warm reception. Col. Fulsom and Lt. Col. Wells were immediately ordered to encircle the grove on the right, wile Gen. Gano, with his brave 500 at a sweeping gallop dashed around to the left. No sooner had the head of our column come within striking distance than the enemy opened upon us with their Sharpe's rifles. It was but the work of a moment for the general to form his men, and with a Texas yell they dashed forward.

The Battle of Massard Prairie

The enemy were a portion of the 6th Kansas, and this is the third time our brigade had fought them. Their force was variously estimated from 300 to 500. They had every advantage of us in position, and fought desperately, more so than usual, as the commanding officer told us afterwards that he thought we were all Indians, and they would every one be butchered so he fave orders to his men not to surrender, but to sell their lives as dearly possible. The fight lasted perhaps half an hour, and although I will not say as some newspaper writers do, that it 'was the bloodiest battle of the war,' yet it was a right gallant little affair, and reflects credit on our gallant commander and his brave men, and terminated in our complete victory. We captured Maj. Mefford, commanding, a lieutenant, and 125.

We captured a large quantity of stores of every description, but owing to the heavy reinforcements coming up from Fort Smith, we only saved what the men could carry on their horses. We were compelled to burn and abandon the balance.

Our loss was 5 killed, and 7 severely, and 2 slightly wounded. That of the enemy between 50 and 60 killed and wounded.

Galveston (Texas) *Weekly News*
August 17, 1864

The Fight at Diamond Grove, Arkansas
Camp 20 miles south of Fort Smith, July 28th, 1864.

We marched through Sculleyville, a deserted Indian village; then took a road leading in a north easterly direction, and got on finely until nightfall. Through the incompetency of our guides and the multiplicity of Indian trains, the brigade got lost. We blundered about until midnight, finally found the road, crossed the Poteau river, and marched to within four miles, as our guides informed us, of the position of the enemy. It was the intention of Gen. Gano to attack them at daylight. At five o'clock we were again in our saddles, but instead of finding the Yankees in four miles, we had to march ten. About six o'clock in the morning we reached Mazzard Prairie (Arkansas) and

Chapter Eight

drove in their pickets. Riding out on the prairie, our advance of Indians had a miscellaneous skirmish with a few adventurous Yankees.

In the centre of the prairie stood a beautiful grove, called Diamond Grove. There the general ascertained the enemy to be encamped. Ordering the Indians and Lieut. Col. Wells to the right, the General, with the detachment of his own brigade, proceeded to the left of the grove in a sweeping gallop. Arriving within three or four hundred yards of the encampment, the General ordered Capt. Welch, of the Gano Guards, to dash into the timber, and, assisted by Capt. Hard's company and a detachment of the 29th Texas cavalry, under Major Carroll, to drive the enemy into the prairie.

He then placed the remained of his command in position to secure the game when roused. These movements were promptly executed. The enemy, 6th Kansas, were drawn up in line of battle in front of their tents. Immediately a hot fight began in the timber. It lasted but a few minutes, when the routed enemy abandoned the timber and fled to the prairie – our fellows at their heels. They fought with desperation under the impression that the Indians would murder them if they surrendered. The fight was kept up on the prairie some fifteen or twenty minutes, when the entire party was either killed or captured, with the exception of 150 mounted men who effected their escape before the grove was surrendered. The killed and wounded between fifty and sixty, captured one hundred and twenty-seven prisoners, sixteen wagons, and a great many sutlers stores. The tents, wagons, etc., had to be burned as they could not be brought out by our tortuous and difficult route. The prisoners are now in camp. Our men had a fine opportunity to supply themselves with pistols, overcoats, and all the luxuries of the Yankee Sutler's establishment. Your correspondent is even now solacing himself with the unwonted luxury of a good cigar. We had scarcely began a retrograde movement before the enemy, in large force, from Fort Smith made their appearance on the prairie. They had a battery with them. Gen. Gano did not think it prudent to fight them without artillery, fatigued as the troops were, so we very, very leisurely retired before them. They followed us very cautiously a few miles, occasionally firing on our rear, but soon drew off. At night we encamped on Poteau river and this morning reached camp.

The Battle of Massard Prairie

Gen. Gano was in the thickest of the fray, directing and cheering the men, and his coolness and gallantry is the theme of the entire brigade. You can always tell his whereabouts by the cheering of the troops. Maj. Stackpole, Cap. Matthews, Lt. Adams and Lieut. Wall of the staff were on the field and rendered valuable assistance. Our loss was 6 killed and 15 wounded. – *Dallas Herald.*

Augusta (Georgia) *Chronicle and Sentinel*
October 5, 1864 (quoting the Meridian *Clarion*)

An account is given of a brilliant little victory that was gained early in August by a party of Choctaw and Texas troops, all under Gen. Gano. The fighting took place five miles S.E. of Fort Smith, in Mesard Prairie. The Lincolnite forces consisting of the "Kansas Sixth" and the so-called home guards. The first has long been a "crack" regiment, alike noted for its ferocity, fanaticism and brutality. Gen. Gano divided his Texans into two bodies, whiles the Choctaws formed a third. One held in person on the center, whilst the others executed a flanking movement on either hand.

Advancing to the summit of an eminence where Yankee balls were whizzing all around him, Col. Folsom prevailed on his Choctaws to accompany him over a broad space to the face of the enemy. The other bodies charged simultaneously, and the robbers finding themselves previously assiled in front and on both flanks, commenced a skedaddle from the rear, whilst others fought with desperation, until assured of quarters, when they surrendered. – Many of our men clubbed with their guns and dealt stunning blows; several guns were in this way broken. One hundred and twenty-seven were captured and about sixty killed. The pursuit was kept up to within two miles of Ft. Smith. The number of the enemy's wounded could not be ascertained. Our men obtained a rich booty – 200 Sharp's rifles, 400 revolvers, hundreds of excellent saddles, a considerable number of over coats and many other things.

Chapter Eight

Macon (Georgia) *Telegraph*
October 19, 1864

FROM THE CHOCTAW NATION.

It is seldom we hear anything about Confederate operations in the Indian Nation. We are glad to see from our Texas files that everything is working favorably there under the direction of able and veteran commanders. The commanding officer of the district is Maj. Gen. Maxey, who long since distinguished himself on the eastern side of the Mississippi. He causes to be published irregularly a bulletin, giving brief notice of the most important events which transpire in the...trans-Mississippi departments. This is the only means which the soldiers and citizens have of knowing what is going on in the country....

Gen. Gano figured with the lamented Morgan and is well known to our readers. Stand Watie is a Cherokee of education and refinement, and before the war enjoyed as much wealth and happiness as his whiter friends in the States. He now has nothing left but his sword and equipments. His life since the commencement of the war has presented almost a continuous series of struggles. Of the Indian Territory he is pronounced decidedly the Mariaon. An account is given of a brilliant little victory that was gained early in August by a party of Choctaws and Texas troops, all under Gen. Gano. The fighting took place five miles southeast of Fort Smith, in Mozard prairie. The Lincolnite forces considered of the 6th Kansas and the so-called home guards. The first has long been a "crack" regiment, alike noted for its ferocity, fanaticism and brutality.

Gen. Gano divided his Texans into two bodies, whilst the Choctaws formed a third. One he held in person on the center, whilst the others executed a flank movement on either hand. Advancing to the summit of an eminence where the Yankee balls were whizzing all around him, Col. Fulsom prevailed on his Choctaws to accompany him over a broad space to the face of the enemy. The other bodies charged simultaneously, and the robbers finding themselves previously assailed in front and on both flanks, commenced a skedaddle from the rear, whilst others fought with desperation until assured of quarter, when they surrendered. Many of our men clubbed with their guns and dealt stunning blows; several guns were in this way broken. One hundred and twenty seven were captured and about sixty killed. The pursuit was kept up to within about two miles of Fort Smith. The pursuit was kept up to within about two miles of Fort Smith. The number of the enemy's wounded could not be ascertained. Our men obtained a rich booty – two hundred Sharp's rifles, four hundred revolvers, hundreds of excellent saddles, a considerable number of overcoats and many other things.

Appendices

Known Confederate Casualties

The Battle of Massard Prairie, Arkansas

Killed:

Capt. C.C. McCurry	Company F, 30th Texas Cavalry
Sgt. Polk Levy	Company A, 30th Texas Cavalry
John Small	Company E, 30th Texas Cavalry
Tiok-homa (Red Pine)	Folsom's Brigade
William Jayroe	Company F, 30th Texas Cavalry

Wounded:

Capt. J.P. Morris	Company B, 30th Texas Cavalry
Capt. Jackson Puckett	Company H, 30th Texas Cavalry
Lt. J.C. Snead	Company H, 30th Texas Cavalry
Sgt. G.W. Jackson	Company B, 30th Texas Cavalry
Asa Johnson	Company A, 30th Texas Cavalry
W.R. Baker	Company F, 30th Texas Cavalry
William Hensley	Company C, 30th Texas Cavalry
W.E. Richardson	Company E, 30th Texas Cavalry
A.J. Wiley	Company F, 30th Texas Cavalry

Known Union Casualties

The Battle of Massard Prairie, Arkansas

Killed:

Corp. George L. Harris	Company I, 6th Kansas Cavalry
Corp. Thomas Landers	Company E, 6th Kansas Cavalry
Corp. Thomas L. McCauley	Company B, 6th Kansas Cavalry
John Parker	Company B, 6th Kansas Cavalry
Joshua B. Zents	Company B, 6th Kansas Cavalry
Albert H. Richley	Company D, 6th Kansas Cavalry
Joel G. Hutchin	Company E, 6th Kansas Cavalry
David Vanwormer	Company E, 6th Kansas Cavalry
James Weldon	Company E, 6th Kansas Cavalry
Daniel Jennings	Company H, 6th Kansas Cavalry
William M. Rice	Company L, 6th Kansas Cavalry

Mortally Wounded:

Thomas Francis	Company D, 6th Kansas Cavalry
Thomas R. Griffin	Company H, 6th Kansas Cavalry
George W. Rinker	Company B, 6th Kansas Cavalry
Benjamin C. Wallace	Company B, 6th Kansas Cavalry

Wounded:

1st Lt. Jacob Morehead	Company B, 6th Kansas Cavalry
Sgt. James H. Asher*	Company B, 6th Kansas Cavalry
Sgt. Charles S. Atkins	Company D, 6th Kansas Cavalry

Corp. Calvin R. Jackson	Company B, 6th Kansas Cavalry
Antoine Furtmire	Company B, 6th Kansas Cavalry
Marion Hinton	Company B, 6th Kansas Cavalry
Edwin Jackson	Company B, 6th Kansas Cavalry
David P. McDonald	Company B, 6th Kansas Cavalry
Edwin Parker	Company B, 6th Kansas Cavalry
Charles S. Atkins	Company D, 6th Kansas Cavalry
John Phillips	Company D, 6th Kansas Cavalry
Peter Bartness	Company D, 6th Kansas Cavalry
James S. Mounce	Company H, 6th Kansas Cavalry
Lewis Pawnee	Company L, 6th Kansas Cavalry
William Patterson	Wagon Master

Captured:

Major David Mefford	6th Kansas Cavalry
James Kirks	Company A, 6th Kansas Cavalry
B.F. Russell	Company A, 6th Kansas Cavalry
James Smith	Company A, 6th Kansas Cavalry
Sgt. Noah Scott	Company B, 6th Kansas Cavalry
Sgt. Addison Pendergast	Company B, 6th Kansas Cavalry
Sgt. John W. Miller	Company B, 6th Kansas Cavalry
Sgt. Cyrus N. Teater	Company B, 6th Kansas Cavalry
Corp. Peter Sidles	Company B, 6th Kansas Cavalry
Corp. David P. McDonald	Company B, 6th Kansas Cavalry
Corp. Oliver C. Rinker	Company B, 6th Kansas Cavalry
Corp. Thomas C. Harrison	Company B, 6th Kansas Cavalry
David H. Allen	Company B, 6th Kansas Cavalry
Sylvester Buck	Company B, 6th Kansas Cavalry
Cyrus Boston	Company B, 6th Kansas Cavalry
Thomas Hamlin	Company B, 6th Kansas Cavalry
Alexander Jackson	Company B, 6th Kansas Cavalry
Edward T. Jennings	Company B, 6th Kansas Cavalry
Adam Kiser	Company B, 6th Kansas Cavalry
Enoch Manning	Company B, 6th Kansas Cavalry

William J. Manning	Company B, 6th Kansas Cavalry
George R. Root	Company B, 6th Kansas Cavalry
Elmore Strickland	Company B, 6th Kansas Cavalry
John O. Wood	Company B, 6th Kansas Cavalry
David S. Clark	Company B, 6th Kansas Cavalry
John Cox	Company B, 6th Kansas Cavalry
Benjamin F. Davis	Company B, 6th Kansas Cavalry
Thomas Haslett	Company B, 6th Kansas Cavalry
Jefferson Kenedy	Company B, 6th Kansas Cavalry
John O. Wood	Company B, 6th Kansas Cavalry
Donald McDonald	Company B, 6th Kansas Cavalry
Edward R. Arrison	Company B, 6th Kansas Cavalry
Samuel J. Bellvail	Company B, 6th Kansas Cavalry
Arthur Gillman	Company B, 6th Kansas Cavalry
John W. Goldsberry	Company B, 6th Kansas Cavalry
Andrew Humphrey	Company B, 6th Kansas Cavalry
William T. Hercules	Company B, 6th Kansas Cavalry
George McGuire	Company B, 6th Kansas Cavalry
Allison W. Orrill	Company B, 6th Kansas Cavalry
Matthew Paite	Company B, 6th Kansas Cavalry
David Paite	Company B, 6th Kansas Cavalry
George W. Ross	Company B, 6th Kansas Cavalry
Josiah Roy	Company B, 6th Kansas Cavalry
Sgt. J.S. Vanbuhler	Company D, 6th Kansas Cavalry
Corp. Joseph G. Cooper	Company D, 6th Kansas Cavalry
Corp. J. Rockhold	Company D, 6th Kansas Cavalry
Samuel Crawshaw	Company D, 6th Kansas Cavalry
Afred Edmiston	Company D, 6th Kansas Cavalry
David Gaines	Company D, 6th Kansas Cavalry
James Harbour	Company D, 6th Kansas Cavalry
George Hensley	Company D, 6th Kansas Cavalry
Marion Holderman	Company D, 6th Kansas Cavalry
Reuben Lamb	Company D, 6th Kansas Cavalry
William Lamb	Company D, 6th Kansas Cavalry
Isaiah Newton	Company D, 6th Kansas Cavalry
Lewis Pierce	Company D, 6th Kansas Cavalry

J. Wiseman	Company D, 6th Kansas Cavalry
2nd Lt. John F. Defries	Company E, 6th Kansas Cavalry
Sgt. John F. Back	Company E, 6th Kansas Cavalry
Sgt. Thomas Lowmans	Company E, 6th Kansas Cavalry
Corp. Charles Hanley	Company E, 6th Kansas Cavalry
Corp. Johnson Petty	Company E, 6th Kansas Cavalry
George Arney	Company E, 6th Kansas Cavalry
John Belmont	Company E, 6th Kansas Cavalry
William W. Caldwell	Company E, 6th Kansas Cavalry
Thomas Carmack	Company E, 6th Kansas Cavalry
Christopher Clapp	Company E, 6th Kansas Cavalry
Isaac Crossley	Company E, 6th Kansas Cavalry
J.A. Davis	Company E, 6th Kansas Cavalry
C. Dedrick	Company E, 6th Kansas Cavalry
J.H. Dorsey	Company E, 6th Kansas Cavalry
J.L. Hasley	Company E, 6th Kansas Cavalry
George Huff	Company E, 6th Kansas Cavalry
W.W. Hutchen	Company E, 6th Kansas Cavalry
Augustus Kelsey	Company E, 6th Kansas Cavalry
Enos Lang	Company E, 6th Kansas Cavalry
John Lang	Company E, 6th Kansas Cavalry
Joseph McDowell	Company E, 6th Kansas Cavalry
Simon McDowell	Company E, 6th Kansas Cavalry
T.D. Noggles	Company E, 6th Kansas Cavalry
John Parton	Company E, 6th Kansas Cavalry
Elias G. Shavers	Company E, 6th Kansas Cavalry
Henry Snyder	Company E, 6th Kansas Cavalry
William Snyder	Company E, 6th Kansas Cavalry
Joseph Stenson	Company E, 6th Kansas Cavalry
Frank Umphrey	Company E, 6th Kansas Cavalry
Richard Vanwormer	Company E, 6th Kansas Cavalry
Edward Venable	Company E, 6th Kansas Cavalry
Thomas Watkins	Company E, 6th Kansas Cavalry
Peter Wilson	Company E, 6th Kansas Cavalry
John W. Woods	Company E, 6th Kansas Cavalry

Appendices

Sgt. Thomas E. Sauls	Company H, 6th Kansas Cavalry
Sgt. Lorenzo Dillender (?)	Company H, 6th Kansas Cavalry
Sgt. Riley Melton	Company H, 6th Kansas Cavalry
Sgt. William A. Medlen	Company H, 6th Kansas Cavalry
Corp. Noel Crow	Company H, 6th Kansas Cavalry
Corp. Ephraim Fry	Company H, 6th Kansas Cavalry
Corp. Francis McComb	Company H, 6th Kansas Cavalry
Corp. J.W. Stoneman	Company H, 6th Kansas Cavalry
Corp. Thomas B. Williams	Company H, 6th Kansas Cavalry
Andrew Anderson	Company H, 6th Kansas Cavalry
Michael Bluton	Company H, 6th Kansas Cavalry
Peter Cowsdine	Company H, 6th Kansas Cavalry
J.J. Dobbins	Company H, 6th Kansas Cavalry
Jeptha Dunkin	Company H, 6th Kansas Cavlary
William Johnson	Company H, 6th Kansas Cavalry
William May	Company H, 6th Kansas Cavalry
William Miser	Company H, 6th Kansas Cavalry
S. Pogue	Company H, 6th Kansas Cavalry
Isaac Secrest	Company H, 6th Kansas Cavalry
Wilson Steel	Company H, 6th Kansas Cavalry
William Wall	Company H, 6th Kansas Cavalry
John Wilson	Company H, 6th Kansas Cavalry
Alfred Dunton	Company L, 6th Kansas Cavalry
Michael McClure	Company L, 6th Kansas Cavalry
Joseph Pierson	Company L, 6th Kansas Cavalry
Stephen L. Rogers	Company L, 6th Kansas Cavalry
James Vices	Company L, 6th Kansas Cavalry
Joseph Pardie	Company M, 6th Kansas Cavalry
Joseph Waller	Company M, 6th Kansas Cavalry

References

Documents

Census of the Choctaw Nation, 1880.
Index to Compiled Military Service Records; Official Army Register of the Volunteer Force, 1861-1865.
Records of the Adjutant General's Office, Wichita, Kansas.
Service and Pension Records of Individual Soldiers, National Archives and Records Administration.
U.S. Census for Benton County, Arkansas, 1860.
U.S. Census for Crawford County, Arkansas, 1860.
U.S. Census for Sebastian County, Arkansas, 1860.

Manuscript Materials

James Robert Barnes, n.d., Accounts of the original Choctaw enrollees.
J.H. Toliver to C.H. Toliver, July 28, 1864, Personal Collection of Pollard Hickman Coates, IV.

Military Records

The War of the Rebellion: a Compilation of the Official Records of the Union and Confederate Armies, Government Printing Office, Washington, D.C., 1880-1901.

Series 1, Volume 1:

Alexander Montgomery, Report of April 24, 1861
Samuel D. Sturgis, Report of May 21, 1861.

Series 1, Volume 22, Part One:

W.L. Cabell, Report of December 7, 1863
William F. Cloud, Report of September 20, 1863.

Series 1, Volume 23, Part Two:

Samuel Curtis to H.W. Halleck, February 10, 1864.

Series 1, Volume 41, Part One:

Douglas H. Cooper, Report of August 10, 1864.
Jacob Morehead, Report of July 29, 1864.
John H. Thayer to Frederick Steele, July 30, 1864.
Itinerary of the District of the Frontier.
S.B. Maxey to W.R. Boggs, July 30, 1864.
Levi F. Stewart, Report of August 2, 1864.

Series 1, Volume 53:

William Burgoyne, Report of July 29, 1864.

Newspapers

Augusta, Georgia, *Chronicle & Sentinel*, October 5, 1864.

Augusta, Georgia, *Chronicle & Sentinel*, October 12, 1864, p. 3, quoting an eyewitness account in the Meridian, Mississippi, *Clarion*.

Augusta, Georgia, *Chronicle & Sentinel*, October 5, 1864.

Augusta, Georgia, *Daily Constitutionalist*, September 25, 1864, transcribed by Vicki Betts.

Leavenworth, Kansas, *Daily Times*, August 7, 1864.

Fort Smith, Arkansas, *New Era*, July 30, 1864, p. 2.

Fort Smith, Arkansas, *New Era*, August 6, 1864, p. 2.

Protest to the editor of the *New Era*, July 5, 1864, reprinted in the Little Rock *Unconditional Union*, August 4, 1864, p. 1, transcribed by Vicki Betts, *Newspaper Research,* 1861-1865. http://www.uttyl.edu/vbetts/.

Galveston Weekly News August 17, 1864, transcribed by Vicki Betts, *Newspaper Research,* 1861-1865. http://www.uttyl.edu/vbetts/.

Houston, Texas, *Telegraph,* August 17, 1864.

Houston, Texas, *Telegraph*, August 15, 1864.

Leavenworth, Kansas, *Daily Times*, August 7, 1864.

Publications

Edwin C. Bearss and Arrell M. Gibson, *Fort Smith: Little Gibraltar on the Arkansas*, University of Oklahoma Press, 1979.

Steve Cox, "The Action on Massard Prairie," *The Journal* of the Fort Smith Historical Society, Volume 4, Number 1, April 1980.

Frank Cunningham, *General Stand Watie's Confederate Indians*, University of Oklahoma Press (Reprint edition), 1998

Tom Wing, Ed., *"A Rough Introduction to This Sunny Land":* *The Civil War Diary of Private Henry A. Strong, Co. K, Twelfth Kansas Infantry*, Butler Center for Arkansas Studies, Central Arkansas Library System, 2006.

About the Author

A native of the quaint Northwest Florida community of Two Egg, Dale Cox grew up immersed in the history and folklore of the American South. He is a descendent of both the Native American leader Efie Emathla (William Brown), a chief of the Yuchi branch of the Creek nation, and the American pioneer Daniel Boone.

His unique cultural heritage played a critical role in forming his life-long love of history and passion for preservation. A trained historian and anthropologist, he has written or contributed to a number of books on U.S. history. His 2007 publication, *The Battle of Marianna, Florida*, was critically acclaimed as a "groundbreaking study of a small battle."

The Battle of Massard Prairie is one of a series of manuscripts written by the author between 1991 and 2007, several of which will be published in coming years. His current books in print include *The Battle of Natural Bridge, Florida* and *Two Egg, Florida: A Collection of Ghost Stories, Legends and Unusual Facts*.

The son of Clinton and Pearl Cox of Jackson County, Florida, Mr. Cox is the father of two grown sons, William and Alan. He divides his time between Fort Smith, Arkansas, and his original hometown of Two Egg, Florida.

Index

111

Other Books by Dale Cox

The Battle of Marianna, Florida

A history of the little known September 27, 1864, engagement that culminated the deepest penetration of Florida by Union troops during the entire Civil War.

The Battle of Natural Bridge, Florida

The new "standard history" of the 1865 battle that preserved Tallahassee's status as the only Southern capital east of the Mississippi not captured by Union troops.

Two Egg, Florida

A fascination collection of the "stories behind the stories" of some of Northwest Florida's favorite ghost stories, legends and unusual facts.

Available at:

www.barnesandnoble.com
www.amazon.com
www.exploresouthernhistory.com

Made in the USA
Middletown, DE
05 December 2016